INTRODUCTION TO CREATIVE FINANCING

THE REAL ESTATE INVESTING
MENTOR
THE AFFORDABLE $50K COACHING ALTERNATIVE

James Orr
The Real Estate Financial Planner™

Published by:

Real Estate Financial Planner LLC
PO Box 2163
Loveland CO 80539

https://RealEstateFinancialPlanner.com

First edition November 2024.
File: 2024-11-15 - Introduction to Creative Financing

This publication is designed to provide accurate and authoritative information regarding the subject matter covered. It is sold with the understanding that the publisher is not engaged in rendering legal, accounting or other professional advice or services. If legal advice or other expert advice is required, the services of a competent professional person should be sought.

From a *Declaration of Principles* jointly adopted by a Committee of American Bar Association and a Committee of Publishers and Associations.

This is a work of fiction. References to clients in this book are fictional and have been modified and changed from any possible real situations to protect the identities of clients and to simplify the stories for clarity. In some cases, significant parts of the stories have been changed. In some cases, stories have been completely fabricated to illustrate a concept. Any similarities to people alive or dead is purely coincidental.

AI Disclosure: While James Orr authored the original version of this content, AI was used extensively to draft, proofread, edit, improve and write subsequent versions and variations.

DEDICATION

Dedicated to my wife Tammy. I have no words.

FREE DOWNLOAD

The World's Greatest Real Estate Deal Analysis Spreadsheet™

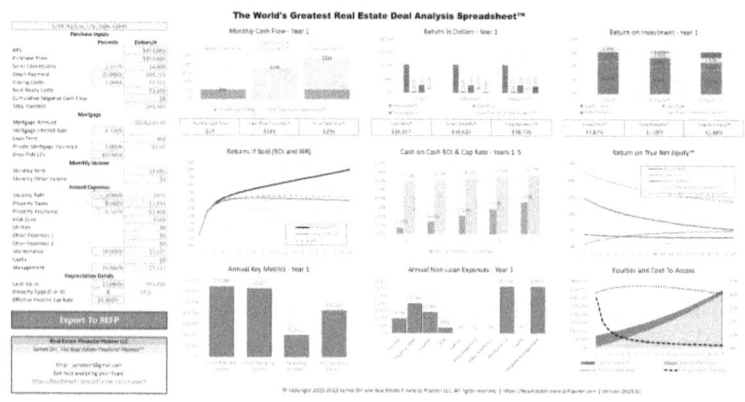

Thank you for purchasing this book and taking the next step toward mastering real estate investing.

As a special bonus, you can download *The World's Greatest Real Estate Deal Analysis Spreadsheet*™ for free. This powerful tool will help you analyze deals like a pro, ensuring you make informed, profitable decisions.

Download your free copy now and start running the numbers with confidence.

https://REFP.com/spreadsheet

Table of Contents

Introduction to Creative Financing

Ready to unlock the secrets of creative financing in real estate investing? You're about to embark on an exciting journey that could revolutionize your approach to property acquisition. Creative financing isn't just a buzzword—it's a powerful set of strategies that can help you bypass traditional bank loans and mortgages.

Imagine being able to invest in real estate with little to no money down, or structuring deals that work for both you and the seller. That's the power of creative financing. Whether you're a seasoned investor or just starting out, these non-traditional methods can open doors to opportunities you might have thought were out of reach.

In this comprehensive guide, we'll explore six types of creative transactions that could transform your real estate investing game. You'll learn about owner financing, wrap financing, loan assumptions, and more. We'll dive into the benefits and potential pitfalls of each strategy, equipping you with the knowledge to make informed decisions.

Remember, with great power comes great responsibility. As we delve into these strategies, keep in mind that the goal is always to create win-win situations.

So, if you're ready to expand your real estate investing toolkit, let's begin.

6 Types of Creative Transactions

Owner Financing	Rent-To-Own, Lease-To-Own, Lease-Option, Lease-Purchase	Wrap Financing
Agreement For Deed, Bond For Deed, Contract For Deed, Installment Land Contract	Loan Assumption	Subject-To

Let's dive into the different types of creative financing options available to real estate investors. Each of these strategies offers unique advantages and considerations:

- **Owner Financing** - In this scenario, the seller acts as the bank. They don't have a mortgage on the property and offer to finance the purchase for you.
- **Wrap Financing** - Here, the seller has an existing mortgage and "wraps" that mortgage by offering you owner financing. It's like a subject-to transaction (which we will cover shortly), but the seller retains the right to foreclose if you don't make payments.
- **Loan Assumption** - With this method, you formally take over responsibility for the seller's loan with the lender's permission. This can be particularly advantageous if the existing loan has a lower interest rate than current market rates.
- **Rent-To-Own Family** - Generically, you're renting the property with the right to be an owner of the property later. These options can be great if you need time to improve your financial situation before purchasing or you're uncertain what the market will do. This category includes these variations:
  - **Lease-Option** - You have a lease agreement with an option to purchase the property.
  - **Lease-Purchase** - Like a lease-option, but with a purchase contract included.
- **Agreement for Deed Family** - This includes variations like Agreement for Deed, Bond for Deed, Contract for Deed, and Installment Land Contract. In these arrangements, you make payments over time, but the deed isn't transferred until you've fulfilled the terms of the agreement. This can be useful for sellers who want

to ensure you can meet the financial obligations before transferring ownership.

- **Subject To** - In this arrangement, you buy the property from the seller, they deed it to you, and you make payments on the seller's existing loan. This can be a powerful strategy, especially if the existing loan has favorable terms.

Remember, each of these strategies comes with its own set of risks and rewards.

It's crucial to thoroughly understand the terms and implications of any creative financing arrangement before proceeding and that's what we will cover here.

Win-Win or No Deal

> *"With great power comes great responsibility."*
> *– Uncle Ben from Spider-Man*

In real estate investing, always aim for win-win deals. It's not just ethical; it's smart business. By ensuring both parties benefit, you build trust, reduce legal risks, and create long-term success. Remember, your reputation is your most valuable asset. If a deal doesn't feel right for everyone involved, be prepared to walk away. There will always be other opportunities that align with this principle.

Benefits of Creative Financing

Let's explore why you might want to consider these innovative approaches:

- **Minimal Down Payment** - Unlike traditional financing that often requires 20-25% down, creative financing can sometimes be done with little to no money down. This allows you to preserve your capital for other investments, additional reserves, improving cash flow or improvements.
- **Bypass Bank Qualifications** - Most creative financing variations allow you to purchase properties without going through rigorous bank qualifications (with a notable exception being loan assumptions). This can be especially beneficial if you have credit blemishes (bankruptcy, foreclosures, short sales) or irregular income. It is a best practice to disclose all material facts about your situation when structuring deals.
- **Flexibility in Ownership Structure** - You can often buy properties in an LLC or other entity upfront, which can provide valuable asset protection and tax benefits.
- **Amplified Returns** - By using less of your own capital, you can potentially see higher returns on your investment. This leverage can significantly boost your wealth-building potential. Be aware though that small down payments and small amounts invested can also amplify losses as well.

- **Exit Strategy Options** - Many creative financing deals offer more flexible exit strategies. If a property isn't performing as expected, you may have more options to walk away compared to traditional financing. For example, rent-to-owns could be structured such that if the market declines during your rent period, you do not need to purchase the property.
- **Retirement Account Investing** - Creative financing can sometimes allow you to use self-directed IRAs or 401Ks to invest in real estate without needing the typical 30-35% down payment or partners.
- **Partnership Opportunities** - These strategies can open doors to partnerships, allowing you to invest in properties without a loan partner. You could work on improving your financial situation (increase income, save down payment, improve credit, establish job history, accumulate tax returns, etc) for future traditional purchases while investing creatively in the meantime.
- **Reduced Capital Expenses Risk** - The nature of many creative financing deals encourages shorter hold times, which can reduce your exposure to major capital expenses (CapEx).

Downsides of Creative Financing

And why you might want to consider NOT doing these types of deals...

Here are some key reasons to consider not using creative financing deals:

- **Limited Selection of Properties** - Buying traditionally allows you to pick from a larger pool of properties on the open market. Creative financing often restricts you to motivated/flexible sellers, potentially limiting your options.
- **More Labor-Intensive to Buy** - Creative deals often require extensive marketing, searching, negotiations and some additional due diligence. This can be time-consuming compared to traditional purchases from within the MLS.
- **Lower ROI for Time Invested** - The effort required to find and structure creative deals may not always justify the returns. Your time might be better spent on other activities or other investment activities.
- **Potential Legal and Ethical Risks** - Some creative financing structures can be complex and may inadvertently cross into questionable legal and ethical territory.
- **Implied Shorter Duration** - Some creative financing implies a shorter time frame. For example, rent-to-own might give a limited time to decide to buy the property.

Jargon Versus General Discussion

For our discussions here, I'll use real estate investing jargon but you should not use jargon when talking to your sellers.

We'll discuss things like:

- **Subject-To** - This refers to buying a property subject to the existing financing.

- **ARV (After Repair Value)** - The estimated value of a property after renovations are completed.
- **LTV (Loan-to-Value)** - The ratio of a loan to the value of an asset purchased.
- **ROI (Return on Investment)** - A performance measure used to evaluate the efficiency of an investment.

However, when you're talking to sellers, it's crucial to switch gears.

Most sellers aren't real estate professionals, so using jargon can be confusing or even intimidating.

Instead, use plain language that anyone can understand.

For example, instead of saying:

"I'll buy it Subject-To and give you $5K for your equity"

You might say:

"I'll buy the house and take care of your mortgage payments. Plus, I'll give you $5,000 at closing."

This approach has two benefits:

- **Clear Communication** - The seller understands exactly what you're proposing without needing to learn new terms.
- **Flexibility** - By using general terms, you're not locking yourself into a specific strategy before you've had a chance to analyze the deal fully and discuss how to structure it with your attorney.

Remember, your goal is to solve the seller's problem, not to impress them with your real estate knowledge. By speaking their language, you're more likely to build trust and close the deal.

Here's another example of how you might approach a seller:

"What if I covered the monthly payments on your loan and took care of the property maintenance so you wouldn't have to worry about that? Is that something that would work for you?"

This simple question could potentially lead to various creative financing strategies, such as a Subject-To deal, a lease-option, or even owner financing. The key is to start the conversation in a way that the seller can easily understand and relate to.

By mastering both the technical jargon for your own understanding and the plain language for seller communication, you'll be well-equipped to navigate the world of creative real estate financing.

You Are Not Your Sellers

Whether or not you would do something is not a reflection of what others would do.

Just because you wouldn't do something doesn't mean someone else wouldn't do it. Just because you would do something, doesn't mean that someone else would do it.

You are not your sellers.

Why Would Sellers Do Creative Financing?

While not a comprehensive list, let's explore some common motivations and why sellers might do creative financing:

- **Solving Financial Problems** - Creative financing can help sellers who are struggling to make mortgage payments or facing foreclosure. It provides a way out of their financial bind while potentially preserving their credit.
- **Quick Property Sale** - For sellers who need to move quickly due to job relocation or other life changes, creative financing can attract more buyers and speed up the selling process.
- **Maximizing Sale Price** - By offering flexible terms, sellers may be able to command a higher sale price than they would in a traditional cash sale.
- **Generating Income** - Owner financing, wrap-around mortgages, and the agreement for deed family of strategies can provide sellers with a steady income stream, which can be particularly attractive for retirees or those looking for passive income.
- **Minimizing Capital Gains Taxes** - Installment sales can spread out the tax liability over several years, potentially reducing the overall tax burden for the seller.
- **Emotional Relief** - For properties associated with difficult memories (e.g., divorce or death of a loved one), creative financing can offer a quicker exit strategy, allowing sellers to move on emotionally.

- **Maintenance Freedom** - Sellers who no longer want the responsibility of property management can use options like lease-purchases to transfer most maintenance duties to the buyer.
- **Market Conditions** - In a buyer's market where traditional sales are slow, creative financing can make a property stand out and attract more potential buyers.

Remember, every seller's situation is unique. As an investor, your job is to listen carefully and structure a deal that addresses their specific needs and concerns while also benefiting you.

Why Wouldn't Sellers Do Creative Financing?

While creative financing can be an attractive option for many real estate transactions, some sellers might be hesitant to engage in these deals. Let's explore some of the reasons why:

- **Not a Good Fit for Their Situation** - Some sellers may need a lump sum of cash immediately for various reasons, such as paying off debts or purchasing another property. Creative financing options that involve payments over time might not meet their immediate financial needs.
- **Fear of Potential Risks** - Sellers may have concerns about:

- ○ **Property Damage** - They might worry about tenants or buyers not maintaining the property properly, potentially decreasing its value.
- ○ **Payment Issues** - There's a fear that buyers might stop making payments, leading to a complicated and costly legal process.
- ○ **Ongoing Involvement** - Some sellers want a clean break and don't want to deal with ongoing financial ties to the property.
- ○ **Social Perceptions** - They might be concerned about what friends, family, or neighbors would think about unconventional selling methods.

- **Unrealistic Expectations** - Some sellers may have inflated ideas about their property's value or market conditions:

- ○ **Overvaluing Their Property** - They might believe their home is worth more than comparable properties in the area.
- ○ **Expecting a Quick, Full-Price Cash Offer** - Sellers might think they'll receive multiple cash offers at or above asking price.
- ○ **Blaming Marketing** - If the property isn't selling, they might think it's due to poor marketing rather than pricing or property issues.
- ○ **Emotional Attachment** - Sellers who have a strong emotional connection to their property might set an unrealistic price based on personal value rather than market value.

- **Preference for Traditional Transactions** - Many sellers are more comfortable with conventional selling methods:

  o **Familiarity** - Traditional sales processes may be well-understood and feel less risky to many sellers.

  o **Quick Closure** - Some sellers prefer the idea of a clean, one-time transaction rather than an ongoing financial relationship.

  o **Professional Guidance** - Working with real estate agents and traditional lenders can provide a sense of security and expert advice throughout the process.

Understanding these potential objections can help you address sellers' concerns and find creative solutions that work for both parties.

Remember, successful creative financing deals often require clear communication, patience, and a willingness to find win-win scenarios.

Owner Financing

Owner financing is a creative real estate strategy where the seller acts as the bank, providing financing for the buyer to purchase their property. This approach can be particularly advantageous for investors looking for alternative financing options.

Here's how owner financing typically works:

- **Seller as the Bank** - The property must be owned free and clear by the seller. This means there's no existing mortgage on the property. If there is an existing loan, it would be considered wrap financing instead.

- **Property Purchase** - You, as the buyer, purchase the property directly from the seller. The transaction is like a traditional sale, but the financing comes from the seller rather than a bank.
- **Negotiated Terms** - You and the seller agree on the terms of the loan. This includes the interest rate, loan duration, down payment amount (and therefore loan amount), payment schedule, and whether there's a balloon payment. You may also negotiate the amortization schedule (for example the loan will pay off over 30 years or 15 years).
- **Legal Documentation** - The agreement is formalized with a promissory note and a deed of trust (or mortgage in some markets) for the benefit of the seller. This provides legal protection for both parties.
- **Ownership and Responsibility** - You become the owner of the property. However, if you fail to make payments as agreed, the seller has the right to foreclose, just like a bank would in a traditional mortgage scenario.

Owner financing can offer flexibility that traditional lenders can't match. For example, you might negotiate a lower interest rate, a longer repayment term, or more favorable qualification criteria.

Some advanced strategies in owner financing include:

- **Substitution of Collateral** - This strategy allows you to potentially swap the property securing the loan with another property, providing flexibility in your investment portfolio.

- **Leveraging Other Financing** - You might use a private money or hard money loan as a down payment, putting the seller in second position. This can help you acquire properties with less of your own capital upfront.

Key Characteristics of Owner Financing Sellers

When you're looking for owner financing opportunities, understanding the characteristics of potential sellers is crucial. Here's what you need to know:

- **Free and Clear Ownership** - More than one-third of all homes in the US are owned without a mortgage. These sellers have the flexibility to offer you owner financing directly.
- **Ability to Pay Off Existing Mortgages** - Some sellers that still have a mortgage may be willing to pay off their current mortgage to offer you owner financing, expanding your pool of potential deals.
- **Motivated/Flexible Sellers** - Look for properties that have been on the market for a long time, are vacant, or aren't being maintained. These sellers may be more open to creative financing options.
- **Out-of-Area Owners** - Sellers who live far from their property might prefer the steady income of owner financing over the hassles of long-distance property management.

- **Income-Seeking Sellers** - Some property owners are looking for a reliable income stream. Owner financing can provide them with regular payments, often at a higher interest rate than they'd get from other investments.
- **Equity-Focused Sellers** - Owners with significant equity in their property might be interested in converting that equity into an income-producing asset through owner financing.

Remember, each seller's situation is unique. By understanding these common characteristics, you'll be better equipped to identify and approach potential owner financing opportunities in your real estate investing journey.

Benefits To Seller of Owner Financing

Owner financing isn't just beneficial for buyers; it offers several advantages to sellers as well. As an investor buyer, understanding these benefits can help you identify motivated sellers and structure win-win deals.

Let's explore why a seller might consider this creative financing option:

- **Quick Sale** - By offering owner financing, sellers can attract a larger pool of potential buyers like you, potentially selling their property faster. This can provide peace of mind for sellers, especially if they've been struggling to sell through traditional methods.

- **Marketing Edge** - Sellers advertising their property with owner financing can make it stand out in a competitive market. This unique selling proposition can attract buyers like you who might not qualify—or want to qualify—for traditional mortgages.
- **Steady Income Stream** - Instead of receiving a lump sum, sellers get regular monthly payments from you. This can be particularly attractive for sellers looking for a consistent income source, perhaps to supplement their retirement.
- **Higher Returns** - Sellers might earn a higher return on their property compared to selling outright and investing the proceeds in low-yield options like CDs or savings accounts. The interest rate on owner financing is often higher than what they'd earn from these traditional investments.
- **Tax Benefits** - Owner financing can offer tax advantages to sellers by spreading their capital gains over several years instead of incurring them all in one tax year. Always encourage sellers to consult with a tax professional to understand how this applies to their specific situation.
- **Flexible Terms** - As the financier, sellers have the flexibility to negotiate terms that work best for them, including interest rates, loan duration, and payment schedules. This can create opportunities for you as a buyer to structure a deal that works for both parties.

Qualifications for Owner Financing

When it comes to owner financing, the qualifications a seller might require can vary widely. It's not a one-size-fits-all scenario, so be prepared for different expectations from different sellers.

Here's what you might encounter:

- **Credit Check** - Some sellers will want to see your credit report, just like a traditional lender. They're looking for a history of responsible financial behavior.
- **Income Verification** - Sellers may ask for proof of income to ensure you can make the payments. This could include pay stubs, tax returns, or bank statements.
- **Down Payment** - The amount can vary significantly. Some sellers might ask for 20% or more, while others might be open to a lower amount or even no down payment at all.
- **Personal Interview** - Don't be surprised if the seller wants to meet you in person. They're entrusting you with their property, so they may want to get a sense of who you are.
- **Property Use Plans** - The seller might want to know your intentions for the property, especially if it's a property they've lived in or have an emotional attachment to.

Remember, these are negotiable points. If a seller's requirements seem too stringent, don't be afraid to discuss alternatives or look for other opportunities. The key is finding a mutually beneficial arrangement that works for both you and the seller.

Owner Financing: Return on Investment

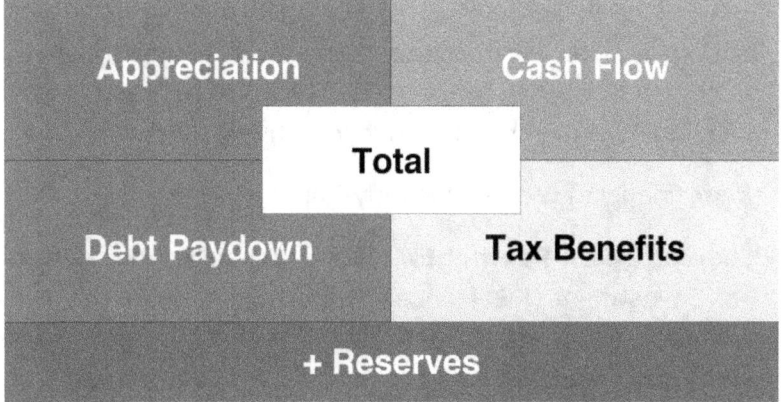

When you invest in rental properties using owner financing, you can potentially amplify your returns. Let's break down the four primary returns you'll earn and how owner financing can impact them:

- **Appreciation** - This is the increase in your property's value over time. With owner financing, you still benefit from appreciation, potentially seeing greater returns due to lower initial investment.
- **Cash Flow** - The money left after paying all expenses. Owner financing can improve cash flow due to potentially lower interest rates and flexible payment terms.

- **Debt Paydown** - As you make payments, you build equity. With owner financing, you might pay down debt faster if terms are more favorable than traditional mortgages.
- **Depreciation** - A tax benefit that allows you to deduct a portion of the property's value each year. You get this benefit with owner financing.

Additionally, you earn a secondary return on the reserves you set aside for the property. This can be interest earned on savings or investments made with these funds.

Owner financing can significantly impact your returns:

- **Lower Down Payments** - This can amplify your Return on Investment (ROI) since the down payment is the denominator in the ROI calculation.
- **Flexible Interest Rates** - Often lower than market rates, improving both cash flow and debt paydown speed.
- **Unique Loan Structures** - Some owner financing deals may have interest-only loans or balloons, which can improve short-term cash flow but may reduce long-term equity building.

Wrap Financing

Wrap financing is a creative real estate strategy where the seller acts as the bank, but with a twist - there's already an existing mortgage on the property.

When you use wrap financing, you're essentially getting a loan from the seller that "wraps around" their existing mortgage. The seller usually continues to make payments on their original loan, while you make payments to the seller based on the new, larger loan amount.

Here's what makes wrap financing unique:

- **Existing Mortgage Stays in Place** - Unlike owner financing, where the property is free and clear, wrap financing involves a property with an existing loan.
- **Two Loans, One Payment** - You make one payment to the seller, who then uses part of that to pay their underlying mortgage and keeps the rest. Although this can be structured differently through negotiations between you and the seller.
- **Flexible Terms** - You and the seller can negotiate interest rates, loan duration, and payment schedules. However, these often need to roughly align with the underlying mortgage to avoid putting the seller upside down.
- **Potential for Lower Down Payments** - Wrap financing can sometimes offer lower down payment options compared to traditional loans.

It's important to note that wrap financing comes with risks. If the seller doesn't make payments on the underlying mortgage, you could face foreclosure even if you've made all your payments. That's why this is sometimes negotiated where you make two payments: one to seller for their portion and one to the seller's original, underlying loan.

Wrap Financing: Return on Investment

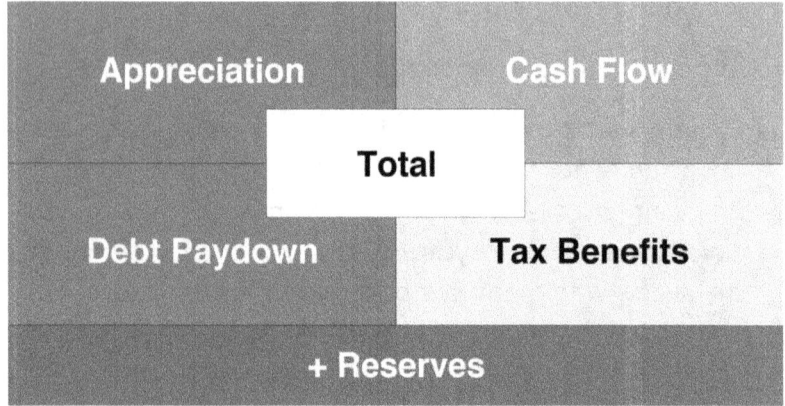

When you use wrap financing, you're tapping into four primary returns on your rental property investment, plus a secondary return. Let's break these down:

- **Appreciation** - This is the increase in your property's value over time. With wrap financing, you benefit from appreciation just like traditional financing.
- **Cash Flow** - The money left after all expenses are paid. Wrap financing can potentially improve your cash flow if you negotiate favorable terms with the seller.
- **Debt Paydown** - As you make payments, you're building equity. There will be two loans (the loan between you and the seller and the loan between the seller and their lender), but you're usually only gaining equity from the loan between you and the seller.
- **Depreciation** - This tax benefit allows you to deduct a portion of the property's value each year, potentially reducing your tax liability.

Additionally, you earn a secondary return on the reserves you set aside for the property. This could be interest earned on savings or investments made with these funds.

The speed and size of these returns in wrap financing can vary. Appreciation and depreciation typically remain consistent with traditional financing. However, cash flow and debt paydown can differ significantly based on the terms you negotiate with the seller.

Remember, while wrap financing shares similarities with owner financing, a key difference is the existing underlying mortgage. The terms of this underlying loan often influence (but don't always dictate) the terms of your wrap loan. This can impact your returns, especially in terms of cash flow and debt paydown speed.

Key Characteristics of Wrap Financing Sellers

When you're on the hunt for wrap financing opportunities, you're looking for a specific type of seller. Let's dive into what makes these sellers unique and how you can spot them.

First off, wrap financing sellers don't own their homes free and clear. In fact, a little less than two-thirds of all homes have mortgages. This means there's plenty of wrap financing opportunities.

Now, what motivates these sellers? Here are some key characteristics to look out for:

- **Long-Time Listings** - Properties that have been on the market for an extended period. These sellers might be more open to creative financing options.
- **Vacant Properties** - An empty house is costing the owner money. They might be eager to find a solution, even if it's not a traditional sale.
- **Out-of-Area Owners** - Managing a property from afar can be challenging. These owners might prefer the steady income of wrap financing over the hassles of long-distance property management.
- **Neglected Properties** - If a home isn't being maintained, it could signal a motivated seller who's struggling to keep up with the property.
- **Pre-Foreclosure Situations** - Wrap financing could be a potential solution for those facing foreclosure, offering a way out of their financial bind.
- **Equity-Rich Owners** - Some sellers might desire a return on their captive equity. Wrap financing allows them to unlock this value as an income stream and, possibly, some cash now from a down payment.

It's important to note that while these opportunities exist, you should always proceed with caution. My attorney, for instance, doesn't recommend wrapping FHA or VA loans. Always consult with your own legal counsel before pursuing any wrap financing deal.

Remember, wrap financing is just one tool in your creative financing toolbox. By understanding the characteristics of potential wrap financing sellers, you'll be better equipped to spot these opportunities and structure deals that work for both you and the seller.

Concerns With Wrap Financing

While wrap financing can be an attractive option for real estate investors, it's important to be aware of potential concerns. Let's dive into some key issues you should consider before jumping into a wrap financing deal.

Underlying Loan Payments

One of the biggest concerns with wrap financing is ensuring that the seller's underlying loan is being paid on time. Here are some strategies to address this:

- **Split Payments** - Consider making payments in two parts: one directly to the original lender for the underlying loan, and another to the seller for their portion. This ensures the original loan is always current.
- **Use an Escrow Service** - You can make payments to a third-party escrow service that will handle distributing the funds to both the original lender and the seller. This adds a layer of security and transparency to the process at a slight additional cost.
- **Seller's Credit Risk** - Remember, if the seller has excellent credit, it's still at risk if payments aren't made properly. This can be a motivating factor for the seller to ensure everything runs smoothly.

Loan Paydown Discrepancies

In rare cases, you might encounter a situation where your wrap loan pays down faster than the original underlying loan. This can happen if the seller's loan is an interest-only loan or has negative amortization. It can also happen if the interest rates are so different that the amortization schedules lead to you paying down your loan faster than they're paying down their loan.

To mitigate these risks, consider the following steps:

- **Due Diligence** - Thoroughly review the terms of both the underlying loan and the wrap loan. Ensure you understand how each loan amortizes and any potential discrepancies.
- **Legal Advice** - Consult with a real estate attorney who specializes in creative financing. They can help structure the deal to protect your interests and address potential issues.
- **Open Communication** - Maintain clear, open communication with the seller throughout the process. Discuss any concerns upfront and establish a plan for handling potential issues.

Qualifications for Wrap Financing

When it comes to wrap financing, you'll find that seller requirements can vary widely. It's not a one-size-fits-all scenario, so be prepared for different expectations from different sellers. Let's break down some common qualifications you might encounter:

- **Credit and Income Checks** - Some sellers will want to ensure you're financially capable of handling the payments. They might request a full credit report, proof of income, employment verification, and bank statements. However, don't be discouraged if your credit isn't perfect. Other sellers may be more flexible, focusing more on your real estate experience or the potential of the deal itself.
- **Down Payment** - This is often a point of negotiation. Some sellers might ask for 20% or more down, while others might be open to a lower amount. In many cases, you might even find a seller willing to do a no-money-down deal.
- **Real Estate Experience** - Sellers may be interested in your track record, including previous successful investments, knowledge of the local market, and property management experience. Don't worry if you're new to real estate investing. Be honest about your experience level and emphasize your dedication to making the deal work.
- **Business Plan** - Some sellers might benefit from knowing your plans for the property and exit strategy. This can build rapport and confidence in your ability to keep your agreements.

Remember, these qualifications are all negotiable. If a seller's requirements seem too stringent, don't be afraid to discuss alternatives or look for other opportunities. The key is finding a mutually beneficial arrangement that works for both you and the seller.

Loan Assumption

Loan assumption is a unique creative financing option that allows you to take over the seller's existing mortgage with the lender's explicit permission. It's a powerful tool in your real estate investing arsenal, especially in markets with rising interest rates.

Here's how loan assumption differs from other creative financing options:

- **Lender Involvement** - Unlike subject-to transactions, loan assumptions require the lender's approval.
- **Credit Impact** - When you assume a loan, it appears on your credit report.
- **Property Ownership** - You become the legal owner of the property, with the deed transferred to your name. This is similar to other creative financing options but differs from the Rent-To-Own and Agreement For Deed families of creative financing strategies.
- **Loan Terms** - Often, you'll inherit the original loan terms, which can be advantageous if the interest rate is lower than current market rates. However, be prepared for potential fees and qualification requirements.
- **Seller's Position** - In most cases, the seller is completely removed from the loan obligation. This clean break can be attractive to sellers looking to move on without lingering financial ties.

Loan assumptions can be particularly attractive in certain scenarios. For example, imagine you find a property with an assumable FHA loan at 3.5% interest, while current rates are at 6%. By assuming this loan, you could save significantly on interest over the life of the loan.

However, keep in mind that loan assumptions often come with challenges:

- **Equity Considerations** - If the property has appreciated, you may need to finance the difference between the assumed loan balance and the purchase price. This might involve negotiating seller financing or seeking additional funding.
- **Qualification Process** - Most assumable loans require you to qualify, similar to applying for a new mortgage. Be prepared to demonstrate your creditworthiness and financial stability.
- **Limited Availability** - Not all loans are assumable. FHA and VA loans are commonly assumable, but conventional loans typically are not.

Loan Assumption: Return on Investment

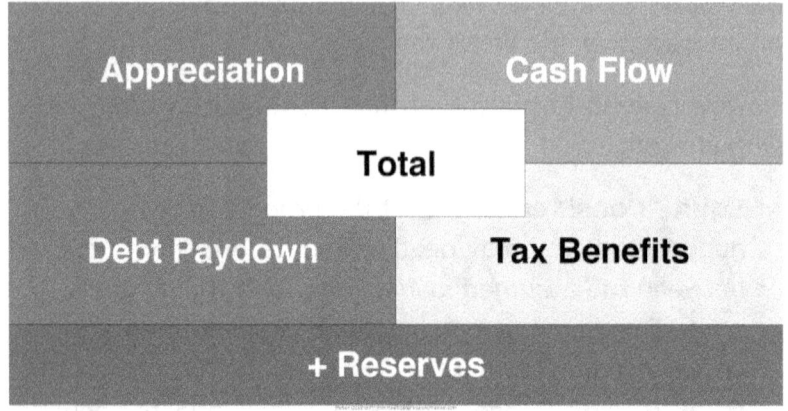

When you assume a loan, you're stepping into the shoes of the original borrower. This means you'll benefit from the four primary returns of rental property investing, plus a bonus return. Let's break it down:

- **Appreciation** - Your property's value may increase over time. With loan assumption, you benefit from any appreciation that occurs after you take over the loan.
- **Cash Flow** - This is the money left after all expenses are paid. Loan assumption can positively impact your cash flow if you're taking over a loan with favorable terms, such as a low interest rate.
- **Debt Paydown** - As you make payments on the assumed loan, you're building equity in the property. The speed of debt paydown depends on the loan's terms and how far into the loan term you are when you assume it.

- **Depreciation** - This tax benefit allows you to deduct a portion of the property's value each year, potentially reducing your tax liability. You'll still enjoy this benefit with an assumed loan.

Plus, don't forget about the secondary return:

- **Return on Reserves** - The money you set aside for maintenance and unexpected expenses can earn interest, adding to your overall returns.

Loan assumption is like owner financing and wraps in that you get appreciation and tax benefits. However, you're formally taking over an existing loan, often with terms like traditional financing.

Here's where it gets interesting: if you finance all or part of the down payment with the seller for their equity (with the lender's permission, of course), your return on investment (ROI) could improve significantly. This is because you're leveraging the seller's equity to increase your potential returns.

For example, let's say you're assuming a $200,000 loan on a $250,000 property. Instead of coming up with the $50,000 difference in cash, you might negotiate with the seller to finance that portion. This could potentially increase your cash-on-cash return and overall ROI.

Remember, always disclose any additional financing arrangements to the lender when assuming a loan to avoid loan fraud.

Key Characteristics of Loan Assumption Sellers

When you're on the hunt for loan assumption opportunities, understanding the key characteristics of potential sellers can give you a significant edge.

Let's dive into how to identify possible loan assumption sellers:

- **Have an Existing Loan** - This is the foundation of loan assumption. The seller must have a current mortgage on the property.
- **Assumable Loan** - Not all loans are created equal. FHA loans are often assumable, making them a strong candidates for this strategy. VA loans can also be assumable, but they come with additional requirements.
- **Owner-Occupancy Requirement** - Here's a potential hurdle: many assumable loans require you to live in the property. This can be a challenge if you're looking to invest, but it opens doors for strategies like Nomad™ or house hacking.
- **Motivated Sellers** - Look for properties that have been on the market for a while. These sellers might be more open to creative solutions like loan assumption.
- **Vacant Properties** - A vacant home is costing the owner money. They might be eager to pass on their assumable loan to avoid further expenses.
- **Out-of-Area Owners** - Managing a property from afar can be challenging. These owners might prefer the clean break that loan assumption offers.

- **Neglected Properties** - If a home isn't being maintained, it could signal a motivated seller who's struggling to keep up with the property.
- **Equity-Rich Owners** - Some sellers might have significant equity due to market appreciation or loan paydown. They may be interested in unlocking this value through loan assumption, but may be more challenging for you coming up with paying out their equity. If the underlying loan being assumed allows for financing of the seller's equity as a second loan, you may be able to negotiate paying out the seller's equity to them over time. Not all lenders will allow a loan assumption with these second mortgages.
- **Attractive Loan Terms** - In a rising interest rate environment, sellers with low-rate assumable loans might ask for a premium. Consider whether paying this premium could still result in long-term savings for you.
- **Quick Sale Desire** - Some sellers might prioritize a faster sale over maximizing their profit. Offering loan assumption could be an attractive option for them.

Remember, if the loan isn't officially assumable, you're in for an uphill battle. You'll need to convince the lender to allow the assumption, which can be challenging if not impossible. It may help to consult with a real estate attorney if pursuing a loan assumption on a non-assumable loan.

By keeping these characteristics in mind, you'll be better equipped to spot potential loan assumption opportunities in your real estate investing journey.

Qualifications to Assume

Loan assumption qualifications vary based on the type of loan and lender requirements:

- **Non-Qualifying Assumable Loans:** These once were the norm. Now, these are extremely rare. No qualification standards apply, simplifying the assumption process.
- **Qualifying Assumable Loans:** Lenders typically use traditional lending criteria. You'll need to meet requirements for creditworthiness, income stability, and debt-to-income ratio.

If the loan maintains recourse against the seller post-assumption, the seller may influence qualification standards due to their ongoing liability.

Communicate clearly with both lender and seller to understand all requirements and negotiate suitable terms.

Seller's Equity

When you're considering a loan assumption, it's crucial to understand how the seller's equity plays into the deal. In many cases, especially in appreciating markets, the seller will have built up equity beyond the loan balance you're assuming.

Here's what you need to know about handling the seller's equity:

- **Down Payment or Monthly Payments** - You'll likely need to compensate the seller for their equity. This can be done either as an upfront down payment or through monthly payments over time.
- **Second Position Seller Financing** - Often, the equity payment becomes a second mortgage, with the seller essentially financing that portion of the purchase. Fully disclose to the first lender to avoid loan fraud.
- **Cash Flow Considerations** - Watch out for negative cash flow when structuring these payments. Adding a second mortgage payment on top of the assumed loan could adversely impact cash flow. However, don't automatically dismiss a deal with potential negative cash flow (which is really just a deferred down payment or financing the down payment over time). Sometimes, the long-term benefits of assuming a low-interest loan can outweigh short-term cash flow challenges.
- **Lender Approval** - Be aware that the original lender may or may not allow a second position loan for the assumption. Always check with the lender before proceeding with this structure.

Types of Loans to Assume

Some loans are better to assume than others. Consider the following:

- **Fixed Rate vs Variable Rate Loans** - Fixed rate loans are generally more attractive for assumption, offering stability and predictability. Variable rate loans can add some additional risk.

- **Fully Amortizing vs Balloon Loans** - Fully amortizing loans are structured so that each payment includes both principal and interest, gradually reducing the loan balance to zero by the end of the term. Balloon loans, on the other hand, require smaller payments during the term but leave a large balance, or "balloon payment," due at the end, often necessitating refinancing or a lump-sum payoff.
- **Long-Term vs Short-Term Amortizations** - Long-term amortizations, like 30-year loans, spread payments over a longer period, resulting in lower monthly payments that improve cash flow but slow equity growth. Short-term amortizations, such as 15-year loans or shorter, have higher monthly payments but pay down the loan balance faster, building equity more quickly and reducing overall interest paid.
- **Low Interest vs High Interest Rates** - Low interest rate loans are highly desirable for assumption, potentially improving your returns significantly. High interest rate loans are less attractive unless you plan to quickly refinance or sell.
- **Qualifying vs Non-Qualifying Assumable** - Non-qualifying assumable loans are rare but valuable, allowing assumption without a full qualification process. Qualifying assumable loans are more common but require meeting the lender's requirements.
- **Seller Recourse** - If you default on the loan, the original seller may still be liable. This can make sellers

hesitant to allow loan assumptions without strong buyer qualifications.

- **Personal Recourse** - Most assumable loans will have personal recourse, meaning the lender can pursue your other assets if you default. Non-recourse loans limiting the lender's claim to just the property are rare but offer more protection for the borrower.

Rent-To-Own Family

The rent-to-own family of creative financing offers a unique approach for real estate investors looking to acquire properties.

- **Rental Agreement with Purchase Option** - You agree to rent the property from the seller while also securing the right to buy it in the future.
- **Flexible Terms** - You and the seller negotiate the details of the agreement, including rent amount, lease duration, maintenance responsibilities, and often the future purchase price. This flexibility allows you to create a deal that works for both parties.
- **Upfront Fee** - Many rent-to-own agreements require an initial option fee. This fee secures your right to purchase the property and may be applied to the purchase price if you decide to buy.
- **Existing Financing Remains** - In most cases, the seller's current mortgage stays in place. This can be advantageous if the existing loan has favorable terms since the seller may not need higher rent to cover their payments.

- **No Immediate Ownership** - As a tenant-buyer, you don't own the property during the rental period. This means less responsibility but also fewer tax benefits compared to owning outright.
- **Variations Available** - The rent-to-own family includes options like master leases and master lease-options.

Compared to other creative financing options, rent-to-own strategies offer a unique middle ground. They provide more control than traditional renting but less immediate commitment than owner financing or subject-to deals.

This approach can be particularly useful for investors who are concerned about how the market may perform in the future. They can lock in some future upside, but significantly limit their potential downside.

Differences

Rent-To-Own or Lease-To-Own is the umbrella term for arrangements where you rent a property with the potential to own it in the future.

This can take two main forms:

- **Lease-Option** - You sign a lease agreement with the option to purchase the property at a predetermined price within a specific timeframe. This gives you the flexibility to walk away if you decide not to buy.
- **Lease-Purchase** - In this case, you have a lease agreement coupled with a purchase contract. This typically implies a stronger commitment to buy the

property at the end of the lease term. Although you may still have clauses in the purchase contract that allow you not to purchase the property.

The choice between these options can significantly impact your rights and obligations:

- **Commitment Level** - Lease-options offer more flexibility, while lease-purchases often come with a slightly stronger expectation to buy.
- **Financial Considerations** - Both may require an upfront fee, but how it's applied can differ. In a lease-option, it's often a non-refundable option fee, while in a lease-purchase, it might be considered earnest money towards the purchase. And, you may have the right to get the earnest money back if you opt not to purchase the property under an acceptable clause in the purchase contract.
- **Legal Implications** - Some attorneys create rent-to-own agreements that combine an option to purchase with a purchase contract that automatically activates when the option is exercised. This hybrid approach can provide greater protection and clarify the overall agreement, but it also introduces additional complexity that requires careful understanding.

Remember, the specific terms of your rent-to-own agreement are negotiable. Tailor them to fit your unique situation and goals.

I strongly recommend having an attorney draft your agreement. Once you've gone through this process with a lawyer, you may feel more confident making modifications to future agreements on your own. However, always proceed with caution when altering legal documents.

Sandwich Lease-Options

Sandwich lease-options are a sophisticated real estate investment strategy that allows investors to control properties with minimal upfront capital. Here's a detailed breakdown of how this approach works:

- **Initial Acquisition** - The investor secures control of a property through a lease-option agreement with the original owner. This could be structured as a traditional lease-option, lease-purchase, or in some cases other creative financing options like owner financing, wrap financing, agreement for deed, or subject-to.

  - When you acquire property with these other creative financing strategies, they're not technically sandwich lease-options, but some investors will refer to them as such.

- **Secondary Lease-Option** - The investor then offers the property to a tenant-buyer on another lease-option basis, creating the "sandwich" structure.

Key financial aspects of sandwich lease-options include:

- **Price Differential** - The investor typically offers the property to the tenant-buyer at a higher price than their agreement with the original owner, creating potential for profit upon sale.

- **Rent Spread** - By charging the tenant-buyer a higher rent than what's owed to the original owner, the investor generates immediate cash flow.
- **Option Fees** - The investor may collect a substantial, non-refundable option fee from the tenant-buyer, which can offset initial costs and provide upfront returns.
- **Negotiated Terms** - The investor can structure favorable terms on both ends of the deal, potentially including extended option periods or specific purchase conditions.

While sandwich lease-options can be lucrative, they come with significant responsibilities and risks:

- **Payment Obligations** - The investor remains responsible for payments to the original owner, regardless of the tenant-buyer's performance.
- **Legal Complexities** - These transactions involve multiple parties and agreements, requiring careful legal structuring and documentation.
- **Market Risk** - Changes in property values or market conditions can affect the profitability of the strategy.

Rent-To-Own: Return on Investment

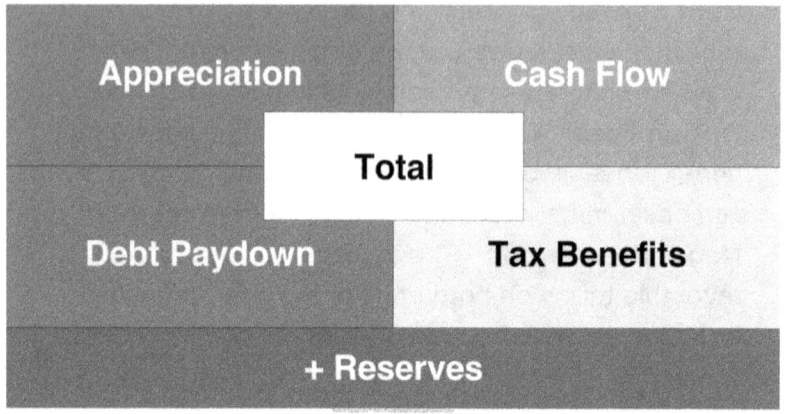

When considering rent-to-own strategies, it's important to understand how they differ from traditional rental property investments in terms of returns. Unlike most other creative financing strategies, except for the agreement for deed family, you don't actually own the property in a rent-to-own arrangement. This unique position affects the four primary returns you typically earn on rental properties:

- **Appreciation** - In a rent-to-own scenario, you might benefit from appreciation, depending on how you structure the deal. If you lock in a purchase price now for a future sale, you could potentially capture the appreciation that occurs during the rental period.
- **Cash Flow** - You may generate some cash flow from the difference between the rent you collect and any payments you make to the seller. However, this can vary greatly depending on the terms of your agreement.

- **Debt Paydown** - In most rent-to-own situations, the seller benefits from the debt paydown on their original mortgage, not you. However, you can structure the deal so that when you buy the property, you pay the seller a fixed amount above their remaining mortgage balance, allowing you to indirectly capitalize on the paydown of their loan.
- **Depreciation** - You probably won't receive tax benefits from depreciation since you don't own the property. This is a significant difference from traditional rental property investments.

Additionally, there's a secondary return to consider; the return on reserves. If you've set aside money as reserves for you might earn a small return on these reserves while they're waiting to be used.

If you choose not to exercise your option/contract to buy, it may be difficult to realize the returns from appreciation and debt paydown. So, unless you exercise your options/contract to buy you're really looking primarily at the return from cash flow only.

The speed and size of these returns in a rent-to-own scenario can vary significantly based on your specific agreement. Appreciation (and possibly debt paydown if you've structured the deal to include that) might be slower to realize but potentially substantial if property values increase. Cash flow could be immediate but possibly smaller than in a traditional rental. The lack of depreciation benefits and debt paydown can impact your overall returns compared to owning a property outright.

Remember, the structure of your rent-to-own deal is important. It determines which of these returns you might access and to what extent. Always carefully consider and negotiate the terms to maximize your potential benefits.

Money Requirements

When it comes to rent-to-own deals, the money required can vary significantly.

- **Flexible Seller Requirements** - Each seller has unique expectations, which can be both an advantage and a challenge for you as an investor.
- **Upfront Money to Seller** - This could be earnest money, an option fee, or a security deposit. Some sellers might request as much as 20% down, while others may treat it like a standard rental arrangement with merely a security deposit. Some may not require an upfront fee at all.
- **Negotiable Rent** - The agreed-upon rent can vary widely. You might find above-market or below-market rates, depending on the seller's situation.

While we've mainly discussed using creative financing strategies to buy properties, sometimes we offer these options to our buyers as well.

A popular approach is offering a rent-to-own arrangement to a tenant-buyer. In this scenario, you'll typically set (or at least compare) the monthly rent to what their mortgage payment would be if they financed the property with their down payment at current interest rates, based on their financial situation.

If the tenant-buyer says they can't afford this monthly rent—which is comparable to what they'd pay with traditional financing—they're essentially telling you they can't afford the home.

What Happens If You Don't Buy?

When entering a rent-to-own agreement as an investor, it's crucial to understand the potential outcomes if you decide not to complete the purchase.

- **Option Fee/Earnest Money/Down Payment** - These upfront payments you make are typically non-refundable. They compensate the seller for taking the property off the market. If you don't proceed with the purchase, you'll likely forfeit this investment. Although, there are exceptions and ways to structure this where this is not true.
- **Monthly Payments** - The rent you've paid isn't refundable, as it was for occupying the property. However, if you've negotiated a portion of your monthly payment as "rent credit" towards the purchase, you may also lose this credit if you don't buy.
- **Repairs and Improvements** - Any repairs or improvements you've made to the property generally won't be compensated if you don't complete the purchase. It's crucial to carefully consider any improvements during the rent-to-own period.

- **Equity Build-Up** - Any equity that has accumulated from paying down the loan typically benefits the seller if you don't buy. Remember, you're not the owner until you complete the purchase.
- **Lease-Option vs. Lease-Purchase** - This distinction is important. With a lease-option, you have the right, but not the obligation, to buy. If you don't purchase, you may only lose your option fee. However, with a lease-purchase, you're typically obligated to buy unless your purchase contract has clauses to the contrary. Breaking this agreement could result in more severe consequences depending on how your paperwork is worded.

Advanced Strategy for Purchase Price

I mentioned this earlier, but let's dive into an advanced strategy for setting the purchase price when you're buying a property on a rent-to-own basis.

This approach can help you benefit from debt paydown in a unique way.

Typically, when you enter a rent-to-own agreement, you and the seller agree on a fixed purchase price upfront. For example, you might agree to buy the property for $300,000 in three years.

But here's where it gets interesting.

Instead of a fixed price, consider negotiating a purchase price that's tied to the seller's loan balance.

Here's how it works:

- **Flexible Purchase Price** - Instead of committing to a fixed price, you agree to pay the seller's remaining loan balance plus a predetermined profit at the time of closing.
- **Seller's Profit** - For example, instead of offering $300,000 when the seller owes $290,000, you agree to pay $10,000 above their loan balance. While the seller's profit is fixed at $10,000, the total purchase price decreases over time as the loan balance is paid down.
- **Benefit from Debt Paydown** - As the seller makes mortgage payments, their loan balance decreases, which directly lowers the total amount you'll pay at closing. This means the longer the seller pays down their loan, the more you save.

You might be thinking, "How much can this actually reduce the purchase price?"

Let's see:

- **Monthly Increase** - The amount of debt paid down increases each month as the loan ages. This is because more of each payment goes towards the principal over time.
- **Interest Rate Impact** - The lower the interest rate on the seller's loan, the more significant the monthly debt paydown.
- **Potential Savings** - For a $300,000 home with a 4.5% interest rate, the debt paydown could be around $4,500 per year. If you hold the rent-to-own agreement for

three years, that's an extra $13,500 profit by structuring the deal this way.

Agreement For Deed Family

The Agreement for Deed family is a unique set of creative financing options that provides financing without up-front, immediate ownership.

Let's explore the variations within this family:

- **Agreement for Deed** - This is the general term for an arrangement where you make payments over time to the seller, but don't receive the deed until all terms are met. Unlike owner financing, you don't get immediate ownership, but you do gain equitable interest in the property.
- **Bond for Deed** - This term is more commonly used in certain regions. It functions similarly to an Agreement for Deed, offering you the opportunity to purchase a property through installment payments without immediate transfer of the title.
- **Contract for Deed** - Popular in some Midwestern states, this variation follows the same principle as an Agreement for Deed. You agree to pay the purchase price in installments, and the seller agrees to transfer the deed once you've fulfilled all the terms.
- **Installment Land Contract** - This name emphasizes the installment nature of the payments. Like other variations in this family, you gain possession and use of the property while making payments, but the legal title remains with the seller until the contract is fulfilled.

These Agreement for Deed variations differ from other creative financing options in several ways.

- Unlike Rent-to-Own strategies, these are considered sales from day one, even though you don't receive the deed immediately.
- They also differ from Subject To transactions, as the seller typically retains legal ownership until all payments are made.
- Compared to Wrap Financing or Loan Assumptions, Agreement for Deed options often don't involve taking over or "wrapping" an existing mortgage. Instead, they create a new financial arrangement between you and the seller.

Agreement For Deed: Return on Investment

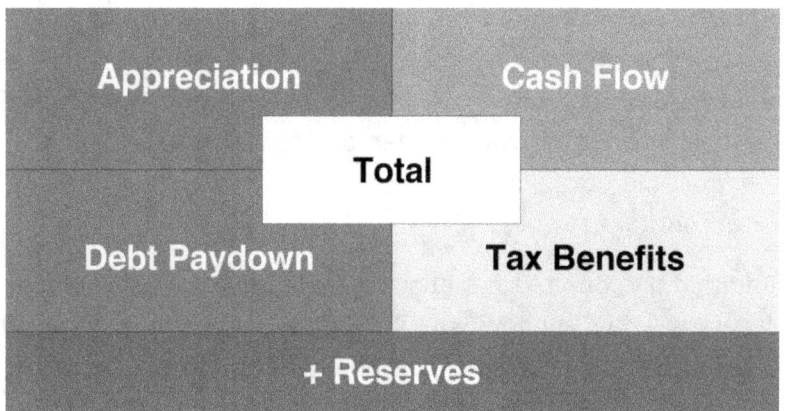

When it comes to the Agreement for Deed family, your returns can vary significantly based on how you structure the deal.

Let's break down the four primary returns you typically earn on rental properties and how they apply to this creative financing strategy:

- **Appreciation** - With an Agreement for Deed, you might benefit from property value increases over time.
- **Cash Flow** - Depending on your agreement, you may generate positive cash flow if your monthly payments to the seller are less than the rent you collect.
- **Debt Paydown** - As you make payments, you're building equity in the property. However, unlike traditional mortgages, you don't officially own the property until you've completed all payments. This makes the debt paydown less tangible in the short term.
- **Depreciation** - Here's where Agreement for Deed differs significantly from other strategies. You probably won't be able to claim depreciation as a tax benefit since you don't technically own the property until all terms are met. Although if you can demonstrate you have equitable title, you may be able to. Talk to your accountant for details.

Additionally, don't forget about the secondary return on your reserves. Any money you set aside for maintenance or unexpected expenses can potentially earn interest, adding a small but noteworthy boost to your overall returns.

Remember, Agreement for Deed is most similar to the Rent-to-Own family in terms of how returns work. Your specific returns will depend heavily on how you negotiate and structure the deal with the seller.

Subject-To

Subject-to real estate investing is a creative financing strategy where you take ownership of a property while the seller's existing mortgage remains in place.

Key points:

- **Property Transfer** - Seller deeds the property to you, making you the legal owner.
- **Existing Loan** - Original loan stays in seller's name, not affecting your credit report.
- **Lender Notification** - Best practice to inform the lender about ownership change.
- **Seller's Credit** - Loan continues to appear on seller's credit report.

Compared to other creative financing:

- **vs. Owner Financing** - Uses existing loan instead of creating a new one.
- **vs. Wrap Financing** - With wrap financing the seller can foreclose and take back ownership of the property if you fail to make payments.
- **vs. Loan Assumption** - No lender approval sought for subject-to.
- **vs. Rent-to-Own** - Immediate ownership transfer for subject-to.

Subject-To: Return on Investment

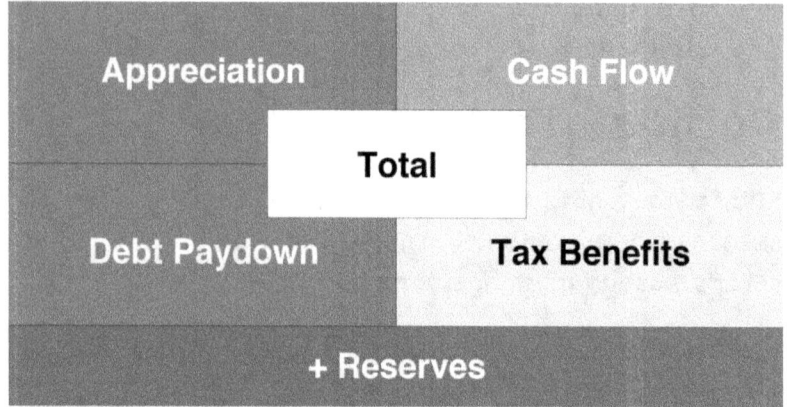

When you use subject-to financing, you're stepping into a unique position that can significantly impact your returns. Let's break down the four primary returns you can expect from rental properties and how they apply to subject-to deals:

- **Appreciation** - This is the increase in your property's value over time. With subject-to, you benefit from appreciation immediately after taking ownership, potentially amplifying your returns if you've invested less upfront.
- **Cash Flow** - This is the money left after all expenses are paid. Subject-to deals can boost your cash flow if you're taking over a loan with favorable terms, such as a low interest rate.
- **Debt Paydown** - As you make payments on the existing loan, you're building equity in the property. The speed of debt paydown depends on the loan's terms and

how far into the loan term you are when you take it over.

- **Depreciation** - This tax benefit allows you to deduct a portion of the property's value each year, potentially reducing your tax liability. You'll still enjoy this benefit with a subject-to deal.

Subject-to financing is similar to owner financing, wraps, and loan assumptions in that you get appreciation and tax benefits. However, you're taking over an existing loan without formally assuming it, which can be both an advantage and a risk.

Don't forget about the secondary return of return on reserves. The money you set aside for maintenance and unexpected expenses can earn interest, adding to your overall returns.

One of the key advantages of subject-to financing is the potential for lower down payments. This can significantly amplify your return on investment (ROI).

Remember, while subject-to can offer attractive returns, it also comes with risks, including the possibility of the lender calling the loan due which we will discuss later.

Creative Financing to...

Creative financing isn't just a standalone strategy—it's a versatile tool that can enhance various real estate investing approaches.

While there are numerous variations, we'll explore a sampling of how you can leverage creative financing to supercharge your investing across different strategies.

- **Long-term Buy and Hold** - Use owner financing or subject-to deals to acquire properties with little money down. This approach allows you to build a portfolio faster, potentially increasing your long-term wealth accumulation.
- **Medium-Term Rentals** - Utilize rent-to-own to rent a property on a long-term monthly rate and then sublet it at a much higher rate as a medium-term rental.
- **Short-Term Rentals** - Similar to medium-term rental example above, maybe you opt to leverage a rent-to-own (lease-option agreement) to test the short-term rental market in a specific area before committing to a purchase. If successful, you can exercise your option to buy using more traditional financing.
- **Rent-To-Own Exit** - Combine the rent-to-own strategy to exit the property with subject-to financing to acquire the property. You can offer rent-to-own terms to your tenants while making payments on the seller's existing mortgage, potentially creating multiple streams of profit.
- **BRRRR (Buy, Rehab, Rent, Refinance, Repeat)** - Use creative financing like owner financing for the initial purchase and rehab phase. Once you've added value and stabilized the property, refinance into a conventional loan to pull out your capital for the next deal.
- **Fix and Flip** - Employ an agreement for deed to secure a property that needs work. This approach can give you

the time to renovate and sell the property without the pressure of traditional short-term loans.

Holding

Let's look at how creative financing performs during your holding period.

Active/Passive

Creative financing strategies in real estate investing tend to be more active than passive.

Here are some reasons why:

- **Upfront Work** - You'll need to invest significant time and effort in finding motivated/flexible sellers and negotiating deals.
- **Deal Structuring** - Each creative financing deal is unique. You'll be actively involved in structuring terms that work for both you and the seller.
- **Ongoing Management** - Depending on how you creatively financed the property and the strategy utilized, you may need to be more actively involved. For example, buying on a rent-to-own requires you to make a decision and complete the purchase later. However, getting 30-year owner financing will be like more traditional financing options.

Duration

When it comes to creative financing in real estate investing, the holding period often depends on the specific strategy you're using.

Let's break it down for each variation:

- **Owner Financing** - This can be a long-term hold strategy. With favorable terms, you might keep these properties indefinitely.
- **Wrap Financing** - Since there is an underlying loan and a risk of the loan being called due, many real estate investors will prefer to either exit the properties within a relatively short period of time or refinance out of the wrap financing. Of course, if the seller's underlying loan is paid off in a short period of time and this converts to owner financing it may change the preferred holding period to indefinitely.
- **Loan Assumption** - This can be a long-term hold strategy like owner financing.
- **Rent-To-Own Family** - These strategies usually have shorter holding periods, often 1-5 years, dictated by the lease term and option period you've negotiated. While slightly less likely to be enforced by the lender, the option part of agreement may also trigger the due on sale or due on transfer clause.
- **Agreement for Deed Family** - If there is underlying financing, this is like wrap financing. If there is not underlying financing, this is like owner financing.

- **Subject To** - Due to potential due-on-sale clause risks, many investors aim for shorter holds, often 2-5 years, using strategies like lease-options to exit.

Remember, these are general guidelines. Your specific holding period will depend on your individual goals and appetite for risk, market conditions, and the unique terms of each deal. Always have a clear exit strategy in mind when entering any creative financing arrangement.

Exit

What are some of the common ways you'll exit out of creatively financed deals? How will your buyers finance them?

Exit Channels

When it comes to exiting properties acquired through creative financing, your exit strategy can vary depending on the specific method you used to acquire the property. Let's break it down for each variation:

- **Owner Financing** - Owner-financed properties offer flexible exit strategies. You can sell traditionally through the Multiple Listing Service (MLS) or For Sale By Owner (FSBO), possibly allowing the new buyer to assume your owner financing agreement. Another option is offering the property on a rent-to-own basis to a tenant-buyer.
- **Wrap Financing** - Exiting a wrap-financed property needs careful planning. You can sell on the open market

via MLS and close out the wrap financing on purchase or, probably more commonly, offer the property on a rent-to-own basis to a tenant-buyer.

- **Loan Assumption** - For properties acquired through loan assumption, exit options mirror traditional financing. You can list on the MLS, sell FSBO, or offer a rent-to-own arrangement. The assumed loan might appeal to potential buyers, especially if interest rates have increased since you assumed it.
- **Rent-To-Own Family** - If you acquired the property through rent-to-own, you might exercise your option to purchase, then use traditional exit strategies. More commonly, you'll use a sandwich lease-option, offering the property to your own tenant-buyer on a rent-to-own basis.
- **Agreement for Deed Family** - This approach offers similar exit options to rent-to-own strategies.
- **Subject To** - Exit strategies here are comparable to wrap financing options.

Exit Financing

When you're ready to exit your creatively financed property, you have several options for how your buyers might finance the purchase.

- **Never Sell** - You might decide to hold onto the property indefinitely. This strategy can work well if you've secured favorable terms through your creative financing, especially with options like owner financing or loan assumption.

- **Rent-To-Own** - You could offer your property on a rent-to-own basis to your tenant-buyers. This strategy can be particularly effective if you initially acquired the property through a rent-to-own agreement yourself, essentially creating a "sandwich" lease-option or with a strategy with a due-on-sale or due-on-transfer risk where you want to limit your ownership period.
- **Traditional Owner-Occupant Loans** - If you're selling to an owner-occupant, they might use conventional, FHA, or VA loans to purchase the property.
- **Traditional Non-Owner-Occupant Loans** - When selling to another investor, they might use investment property loans. These typically require larger down payments and have slightly higher interest rates compared to owner-occupant loans.
- **Cash** - Some buyers, particularly investors, might offer to purchase your property with cash. This can lead to a quicker, smoother transaction, which can be advantageous if you need to exit the investment rapidly.
- **Owner Financing** - If you've built up significant equity in the property by paying off your mortgage, you might consider offering owner financing to your buyer. This can be an attractive option if you're looking for long-term income and are willing to take on the role of the lender.
- **Assumption of Your Creative Financing** - In some cases, particularly when you used assumable loans or owner financing to acquire the property, your buyer might be able to step into your shoes and take over the

existing financing arrangement. This can be appealing in a rising interest rate environment.

Investor/Entrepreneur

When it comes to creative financing in real estate, you're often walking the line between being a Real Estate Investor and a Real Estate Entrepreneur. Let's break this down to help you understand where you might fall on this spectrum.

- As a **Real Estate Investor**, your primary focus is on investing money to generate returns. You're looking at properties as assets that can appreciate over time and provide cash flow. This approach often involves more traditional financing methods and a more hands-off management style.
- On the other hand, a **Real Estate Entrepreneur** is more actively involved in the process. You're not just investing money, but also a significant amount of time and effort. With Creative Financing, you're firmly in this entrepreneurial camp.

Here's why:

- **Time Investment** - You'll spend considerable time searching for deals, negotiating with sellers, and structuring creative financing arrangements. This isn't a passive activity; it requires your active engagement.
- **Marketing Efforts** - To find creative financing opportunities, you often need to market directly to motivated sellers. This marketing aspect is a key entrepreneurial activity.

- **Deal Structuring** - Each creative financing deal is unique. You'll need to craft win-win solutions that work for both you and the seller.
- **Problem-Solving Skills** - Creative financing often involves solving important, often painful problems for sellers. This requires entrepreneurial thinking and the ability to see opportunities and creative solutions where others might not.

Remember, while creative financing leans heavily towards entrepreneurship, it doesn't mean you're not investing money at all as we'll discuss next.

Money Required

What funds are necessary for creative financing deals? What are the most common financial requirements, and what are some of the less common, more unusual monetary needs?

Most Common

While creative financing often allows for low or no down payment deals, there are still several common expenses you'll need to consider.

They are:

- **Marketing Costs** - To find motivated or flexible sellers open to creative financing, you'll likely need to invest in marketing.
- **Down Payment** - While some creative financing deals can be structured with no money down, having funds

available for a down payment increases your options. Some sellers may require a down payment to feel more secure about the transaction or to solve what is making them motivated. The more you can offer, the more deals you'll be able to structure.

- **Closing Costs** - Even with creative financing, you'll still encounter closing costs. These may include attorney fees for drafting the correct creative financing paperwork, title searches, and recording fees. Be prepared to cover these expenses or negotiate with the seller to share them.
- **Rent Ready Costs** - Properties acquired through creative financing may need some work before they're ready to rent. Set aside funds for repairs, cleaning, and any necessary upgrades to make the property attractive to potential tenants.
- **Cumulative Negative Cash Flow** - In some creative financing deals, especially those with little to no money down, you might experience negative cash flow initially. This is essentially a deferred down payment since if you put more down you wouldn't have it. Calculate the total amount of negative cash flow you're likely to accumulate before rents rise enough to make it positive, and be prepared to cover this shortfall.
- **Reserves** - Aim to have at least six months of reserves for each property. This cushion helps you handle unexpected expenses, vacancies, or market fluctuations without putting your investment at risk. Remember, each property should have its own reserves – don't count on using reserves from one property to cover expenses for another.

Less Common

While the most common money requirements for creative financing deals are typically related to down payments, closing costs, and reserves, there are some less common and more unusual ways you might need to use money in these transactions. Let's explore a few of these options:

- **Using Option Fees from Tenant-Buyers** - When selling via a rent-to-own, you might collect option fees from your tenant-buyers. These fees can sometimes be used to offset your initial costs like marketing to find the deal and more.
- **Putting More Down or Buying All Cash** - While creative financing often focuses on low or no money down deals, sometimes putting more money down can lead to better terms. For instance, in an owner financing deal, offering a larger down payment might convince a hesitant seller to agree to more favorable interest rates or a longer repayment period.
- **Converting Creative Financing to Traditional Financing** - You might need funds to refinance a creatively financed property into a conventional loan. This could involve paying for an appraisal, covering closing costs, or even putting additional money down to meet loan-to-value requirements set by traditional lenders.
- **Substituting Collateral** - In some creative financing arrangements, you may have the option to replace the property serving as collateral with another property of equal or greater value. This advanced strategy can be

incredibly powerful for investors, allowing you to free up an existing property for other purposes, such as selling it or using it to secure additional financing. By substituting collateral, you maintain the original loan terms while increasing your flexibility to manage and optimize your portfolio.

Credit Required

When it comes to creative financing in real estate investing, your credit requirements can vary widely depending on the specific strategy you're using. Let's break it down:

- **Seller Flexibility** - Many sellers offering creative financing options won't require good credit. They're often more interested in solving their problem (like selling a property quickly) than in your credit score.
- **Owner Financing and Wrap Financing** - These strategies typically don't involve traditional lenders, so credit requirements are usually more flexible. The seller might ask to see your credit report, but they're often willing to work with less-than-perfect credit.
- **Loan Assumption** - This is where your credit score becomes crucial. To formally assume a loan, you'll need to meet the lender's credit requirements, which are often like those for a new mortgage.
- **Rent-To-Own and Agreement for Deed** - Initial credit requirements are often lenient, but remember: if you plan to obtain traditional financing to complete the purchase at the end of the rent-to-own term, you'll need to meet standard credit requirements at that time.

- **Subject To** - Although credit checks are not usually required for the initial transaction, it's important to understand the risk of the lender invoking the due-on-sale clause if they discover the property transfer. This clause allows the lender to demand full repayment of the mortgage, potentially requiring you to refinance the loan quickly—typically within 30 days—which would likely necessitate good credit.

Remember, while creative financing can offer more flexibility with credit requirements, it's always beneficial to maintain and improve your credit score. It gives you more options and potentially better terms in your real estate investing journey.

Skills Required

Creative financing in real estate investing requires a specific skill set. Here are the primary skills you'll need to develop:

- **Marketing to Find Flexible/Motivated Sellers** - This skill is important for sourcing deals. You'll need to master various marketing techniques to reach potential sellers who might be open to creative financing options.
- **Deal Structuring** - Once you've identified a motivated/flexible seller, you must be able to craft a deal that benefits both parties. This involves understanding various creative financing options and knowing when to apply each strategy to solve specific seller challenges and pain points.
- **Deal Analysis** - Not every creative deal is profitable. You need to develop a keen eye for analyzing potential investments, including cash flow projections, repair cost

estimates, and return calculations under different scenarios.

- **Property Management** - Understanding tenant screening, maintenance issues, and local landlord-tenant laws is essential. You can gain these skills or hire a professional property manager that has these skills.

These skills are developed through continuous learning, practical experience, and sometimes, learning from setbacks.

Stability

When it comes to real estate investing, stability is a key factor to evaluate.

Shane Parrish, the founder of Farnam Street and a thought leader on decision-making and mental models, introduces the concept of active versus passive stability. This framework helps investors assess how much effort is required to maintain a stable investment.

Active stability demands continuous involvement to keep things running smoothly, while passive stability maintains itself with little intervention.

Applying this idea to real estate investing, strategies like creative financing often lean toward active stability, requiring more hands-on management and problem-solving compared to traditional approaches.

Here's why:

- **Shorter Durations** - Many creative financing deals have shorter timeframes, requiring you to stay on top of deadlines and exit strategies.
- **Non-permanent Financing** - Strategies like subject-to deals often involve taking over existing mortgages, which can be called due at any time. You'll need to be prepared to refinance or sell quickly if necessary.
- **Balloon Payments** - Some creative financing options may include balloon payments, where a large sum is due at the end of the loan term. You'll need to actively plan for this eventuality.
- **Interest-Only Loans** - These require careful cash flow management and a solid exit strategy, as you're not building equity through principal payments.

While creative financing is on the more active end of the spectrum, it's important to note that real estate investing, in general, is also actively stable. So, don't expect other real estate investing strategies to be completely passive either.

Scalability

Creative financing can be a powerful tool for scaling your real estate investment portfolio. Let's explore how it compares to other strategies and its potential for growth.

One of the most significant advantages of creative financing is its ability to conserve your capital. Here's why:

- **Lower Down Payments** - Unlike traditional financing that often requires 20% down, creative financing deals can be structured with much smaller down payments, sometimes even zero down. This allows you to acquire more properties with the same amount of capital.

- **Marketing Cost Recovery** - When using strategies like lease options, you can often recoup your marketing costs through tenant-buyer option fees. This helps offset your initial expenses and improves your overall return on investment.
- **Favorable Interest Rates** - In many creative financing deals, you may be able to negotiate better interest rates than those offered by traditional lenders. This can lead to improved cash flow, making it easier to scale your portfolio.
- **Minimal Transaction Costs** - Creative financing often involves lower transaction costs compared to traditional purchases.

However, it's important to note that creative financing isn't without its limitations:

- **Time Constraints** - Finding and negotiating creative financing deals can be time-consuming. As you scale, this could become a bottleneck.
- **Deal Availability** - The availability of sellers willing to consider creative financing can vary widely based on your market. This includes both the geographic location and the market's supply and demand dynamics. In some areas, this may make it difficult to find suitable deals, potentially limiting how quickly you can scale your portfolio.

To overcome these limitations and maximize scalability, consider the following strategies:

- **Build a Team** - As you grow, consider hiring employees or contractors to help with deal sourcing, negotiations, and property management. This can help you overcome time constraints and scale more effectively.
- **Diversify Your Approach** - While focusing on creative financing, don't neglect other strategies. A mix of creative and traditional deals can provide a more robust foundation for scaling.
- **Leverage Technology** - Use software and automation tools to streamline your processes, from deal analysis to tenant screening. This can help you manage a larger portfolio more efficiently.

Risk Exposure

When it comes to creative financing in real estate, you're navigating a landscape filled with both opportunities and potential pitfalls. While these strategies can be incredibly powerful, it's crucial to understand the risks involved. Let's dive into the key risk exposures you should be aware of when considering creative financing deals.

Overall, creative financing carries a medium risk rating. This means that while there are significant potential rewards, you need to approach these deals with caution and thorough due diligence.

Here are the main risks you should consider:

- **Marketing Costs** - Finding creative financing deals often requires extensive marketing efforts. You might need to invest in direct mail campaigns, online advertising, and other marketing to connect with flexible and/or motivated sellers.
- **Amplified Returns** - Creative financing often involves smaller down payments, which can lead to amplified returns - both positive and negative. While this leverage can boost your profits in a rising market with great cash flow, it also means you're more vulnerable to losses if property values and/or rents decline. It's essential to carefully consider your risk tolerance before pursuing highly leveraged deals.
- **Negative Cash Flow Risk** - With smaller down payments, you're more likely to experience negative cash flow, especially in the early stages of your investment. This is essentially a deferred down payment. If you had put more down, you wouldn't have negative cash flow. While it can be mitigated through negotiating better interest rates or more flexible terms, you need to be prepared for potential short-term negative cash flow.
- **Market Volatility** - Creative financing deals are often more sensitive to market fluctuations. A decline in property values or rental rates during your ownership period can significantly impact your investment's profitability.
- **Due on Sale Clause** - Many creative financing strategies can trigger the "due on sale" clause in existing mortgages. If the lender discovers the property transfer, they might demand immediate repayment of

the loan, potentially forcing you to refinance or sell the property quickly.

- o The "due on sale" or "due on transfer" risk comes from changing ownership or equitable title in a property that has an underlying loan from a traditional lender that has a "due on sale or "due on transfer" clause in the note. Since we define owner financing as when the seller does not have a loan, we don't have any concern for "due on sale" risk on owner financing. And, since you're getting the lender's permission with loan assumption, we're not concerned about loan assumption either. However, all the other strategies—wrap financing, rent-to-own family, agreement for deed family and subject-to—all include either a transfer of title or equitable title (like an option) on the property and trigger the "due on sale" or "due on transfer" clause.
- o Historically, while lenders have the legal right to enforce the "due on sale" clause when ownership or equitable title is transferred, most have not exercised this option unless the loan is in default or poses a significant risk to them. In many cases, as long as payments are made on time and in full, lenders have little incentive to accelerate the loan due to the potential complexities involved. However, this is not a guarantee, and enforcement can vary based on lender policies, economic conditions, or other factors. While the probability of enforcement has been historically low, the consequences—such as needing to refinance, sell the property, or pay off the loan in

full—can be severe, making it critical for investors to plan contingencies carefully.

- **Credit Risk** - Certain creative financing methods, like loan assumptions, can put your personal credit at risk. If you fail to make payments, it could severely damage your credit score, impacting your ability to secure future financing.

- **Legal and Ethical Risks** - Creative financing deals can be complex, and if not structured properly, you might inadvertently cross into questionable legal or ethical territory. Always consult with a real estate attorney familiar with creative financing to ensure your deals are structured properly.

- **Property Management Challenges** - Like any real estate investment, you'll face typical tenant and property management risks. However, these can be amplified in creative financing deals, particularly in rent-to-own scenarios where tenant-buyers might have different expectations than traditional renters.

- **Landlord-Seller Noncompliance** - In a sandwich lease-option or agreement for deed arrangement, there's a risk that your landlord-seller may refuse or delay allowing you to exercise your option or complete the purchase agreement. This can create a significant problem if your tenant-buyer is ready to exercise their option or purchase contract with you. If the seller drags their feet or outright refuses to cooperate, you could find yourself in a situation where your tenant-buyer is prepared to buy, but you don't yet hold the title to transfer to them, potentially leaving you unable to fulfill your obligations.

Profit Speed

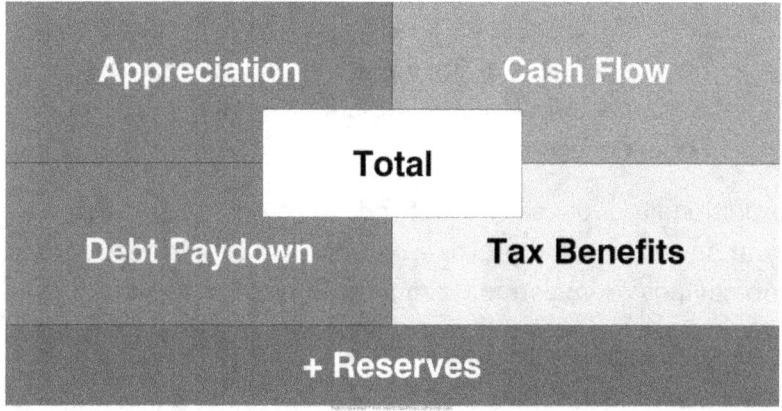

When you invest in rental properties using creative financing, you're tapping into four primary returns plus a secondary return.

Let's break these down and see how creative financing, in general and depending on the specific strategy, can impact them:

- **Appreciation** - This is the increase in your property's value over time. With creative financing, you often still benefit from appreciation, potentially seeing greater returns due to lower initial investment.
- **Cash Flow** - The money left after paying all expenses. Creative financing can significantly improve cash flow due to potentially lower interest rates and flexible payment terms.

- **Debt Paydown** - As you make payments, you build equity. With creative financing, you might pay down debt faster if terms are more favorable than traditional mortgages.
- **Depreciation** - A tax benefit that allows you to deduct a portion of the property's value each year. You get this benefit regardless of financing method, but it can be more impactful with creative financing due to potentially lower initial costs.

Additionally, you earn a secondary return on the reserves you set aside for the property. This can be interest earned on savings or investments made with these funds.

The speed and size of these returns in creative financing can vary significantly:

- **Immediate Profits** - With creative financing, you often see profits immediately. Rents, option fees, or security deposits are typically paid upfront, providing instant cash flow.
- **Amplified Returns** - Due to lower initial investments, your percentage returns like cash-on-cash return on investment can be significantly higher.
- **Flexible Cash Flow** - Depending on your strategy (e.g., long-term rentals vs. short-term rentals), your cash flow can vary from steady monthly income to larger, less frequent payouts.

Remember, your profits can vary widely depending on your specific creative financing strategy and exit plan. For example:

- **Owner-Financing for Long-Term Rentals** - You might see steady, growing cash flow over time as you benefit from potentially lower interest rates and flexible terms.
- **Subject-To for Short-Term Rentals** - Acquire the property creatively and get higher cash flow by utilizing a short-term rental strategy.
- **Sandwich Lease-Options** - You could benefit from immediate option fees, monthly cash flow spread, and potential lump sum profits at the end of the option period.

Lastly, don't forget about *Cash Flow from Depreciation™*. This can provide additional cash flow with each paycheck by adjusting your tax withholdings, or as a lump sum at the end of the year in tax savings.

Creative financing can be a powerful tool to amplify your returns in real estate investing. By understanding these different returns and how they interact with various creative financing strategies, you can make more informed decisions and potentially accelerate your path to financial freedom through real estate.

Finding Deals

How do you find these creative financing deals?

Most Common Methods

Finding creative financing deals often requires looking beyond traditional listings.

Here are the primary methods for finding creative finance deals:

- **Actively Marketed FSBOs -** Properties advertised directly by owners, often found on websites or with yard signs.
- **Hidden FSBOs -** Potential sellers not actively marketing their properties. Uncovered through targeted marketing and networking.

More Unusual Methods

While most creative financing deals come from motivated sellers, two less common methods are:

- **Wholesalers** - Real estate professionals who find off-market properties at discounted prices. Some may have deals with creative financing.
- **Multiple Listing Service (MLS)** - Occasionally, you can find creative financing opportunities here, especially loan assumptions and owner financing.

Finding Creative Financing Deals

Finding creative financing deals means connecting with the right sellers—motivated and flexible individuals who are open to exploring unconventional selling methods and willing to work with you to find mutually beneficial solutions.

The key to achieving this lies in one word: marketing.

Marketing is your most powerful tool for uncovering creative financing opportunities. It's about crafting and delivering a message that resonates with potential sellers.

How you execute your marketing strategy will depend on your resources, goals, and personal preferences. Let's explore the methods you can use to find these deals.

Lazy Marketing Methods

While these methods require financial investment, they are strategically efficient approaches to sourcing deals. By allocating resources to targeted marketing efforts, investors can effectively attract potential sellers without expending excessive personal time and energy.

Lazy marketing methods like:

- **Direct Mail Campaigns** - Send targeted mailings to potential sellers. This could include postcards, letters, or even handwritten notes for a personal touch.

- **Outsourced Door-to-Door Marketing** - Hire someone to distribute flyers in targeted neighborhoods.
- **Pay-Per-Click (PPC) Advertising** - Use online ads to target people searching for phrases like "sell my house fast" or "need to sell home quickly."
- **Search Engine Optimization (SEO)** - Optimize your website to rank for keywords related to selling homes quickly or creatively.
- **Billboard Advertising** - Place eye-catching billboards in high-traffic areas.
- **Radio or TV Ads** - While more expensive, these can reach a wider audience.
- **Print Ads** - Consider placing ads in local print publications.

Poor Marketing Methods

If you're short on cash but long on time and energy, these "poor" marketing methods might be right up your alley. They require more personal effort but can be just as effective.

Poor marketing methods like:

- **DIY Door-to-Door Flyers** - Distribute flyers yourself.
- **Door Knocking** - Take it a step further and knock on doors in targeted neighborhoods. Be prepared with a quick pitch and leave behind information if no one's home.
- **Cold Calling** - Call for sale by owner properties.

- **Driving for Dollars** - Drive around looking for properties that appear vacant or in disrepair. Note the addresses and reach out to the owners.
- **Online Listings** - Post ads on websites or local community forums.

Remember, the key to success in finding creative financing deals is persistence and consistency. Whether you choose "lazy" or "poor" marketing methods (or a combination of both), stick with it. The more potential sellers you reach, the higher your chances of finding that perfect creative financing opportunity.

Analyzing Deals

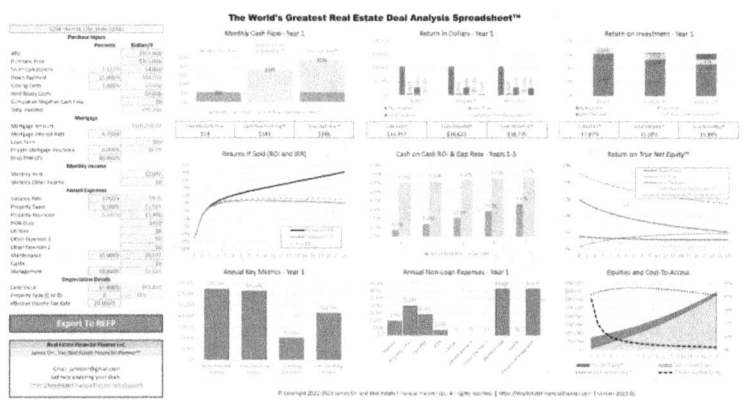

The *World's Greatest Real Estate Deal Analysis Spreadsheet™* is an essential tool for evaluating creative financing opportunities. This powerful spreadsheet allows you to input various deal parameters and quickly assess potential returns.

By using this tool, you can compare different creative financing structures side-by-side, helping you make informed investment decisions. Don't let complex calculations hold you back from pursuing creative deals.

Download your free copy of the spreadsheet now and start analyzing your creative financing opportunities with confidence:

https://REFP.com/spreadsheet

Market Conditions

There are some markets that are better for creative financing deals than others.

Ideal

The ideal market conditions include:

- **Markets with Motivated Sellers** - Look for areas where property owners are facing challenges you can solve. These could be sellers dealing with financial distress, inherited properties, or those needing to relocate quickly.
- **Favorable Price-to-Rent Ratios** - Seek markets where property prices are relatively low compared to potential rental income. This ensures better cash flow and potentially higher returns on your investment.
- **Strong Appreciation Potential** - Target areas showing signs of growth, such as improving infrastructure,

incoming businesses, or urban development. These factors often lead to property value increases over time.

Challenging

The more challenging market conditions include:

- **Hot Seller's Markets** - In extremely strong seller's markets, property owners can often sell quickly and easily for top dollar, even if their properties are in poor condition. This scenario makes it challenging to negotiate creative financing terms, as sellers have little incentive to be flexible.
- **Poor Price-to-Rent Ratios** - Markets with unfavorable price-to-rent ratios can make creative financing deals less attractive. When property prices are high relative to potential rental income, it becomes harder to generate positive cash flow, a key consideration in many creative financing strategies.
- **Stagnant or Declining Markets** - Areas with no appreciation or, worse, negative appreciation in both property values and rents can pose significant risks. In these markets, the potential for long-term gains is limited, which can make creative financing less appealing to both buyers and sellers.

Accessibility/Availability

When it comes to creative financing deals, you'll need to put in some effort to find them.

These opportunities aren't always readily available in the MLS, but with consistent effort and the right approach, you can uncover then.

- **Aggressive Marketing** - Finding creative financing deals at any scale typically requires you to actively market to potential sellers.
- **MLS Opportunities** - While less common, you may occasionally stumble upon owner financing or loan assumption deals in the Multiple Listing Service (MLS). Keep an eye out for these listings, as they can be valuable opportunities.
- **Investor Advertisements** - Other investors might advertise rent-to-own deals or other creative financing options to attract tenant-buyers or buyers. In some less common cases these can be potential opportunities for you to step in as an investor.
- **Direct Seller Interactions** - More often than not, you'll need to directly engage with flexible or motivated sellers to structure creative financing deals. Building relationships and understanding sellers' needs is key to success in this area.

Remember, persistence is crucial.

While these deals might not be as readily available as traditional purchases, the potential benefits make the extra effort worthwhile.

Stay proactive, and you'll increase your chances of finding these unique investment opportunities.

Using Retirement Account

Self-directed retirement accounts are powerful tools for creative real estate financing. These accounts—including self-directed IRAs and 401Ks—allow investments in various real estate deals, offering flexibility and potential tax benefits. However, strict IRS regulations limit the work you can do on these deals. Additionally, you can't use self-directed retirement funds to purchase properties you plan to occupy yourself.

Fees Collected from Your Tenant-Buyer

When selling a property on a rent-to-own basis, you'll typically collect upfront fees from your tenant-buyer. These fees, often in the form of option fees or earnest money, can be viewed in several ways:

Most commonly, the upfront fees you collect will be applied as a down payment when the tenant-buyer purchases the property from you. In essence, you're receiving a portion of your profit upfront.

- **Rebate on Acquisition Costs** - Some investors see these upfront fees as a way to offset acquisition costs, including marketing expenses, down payments, and closing fees.
- **Improved Cash Flow** - Others view these fees as enhanced cash flow, effectively boosting their monthly returns. For instance, a $6,000 down payment for a

year-long lease-purchase could be considered an extra $500 per month in cash flow.

- **Enhanced Security Deposit** - These fees can also serve as an enhanced security deposit, providing financial protection against potential tenant-related issues.

Your approach to these upfront fees will ultimately depend on your investment goals, financial situation, and risk tolerance.

Conclusion

By mastering techniques like owner financing, wrap financing, loan assumption, the rent-to-own family (including lease-option and lease-purchase), the agreement for deed family (including bond for deed, contract for deed, and installment land contract), and subject-to deals, you're expanding your toolkit and increasing your chances of success. Remember, every deal is unique, and having a diverse set of financing options at your disposal can be a game-changer.

Start small, educate yourself thoroughly, and always prioritize win-win scenarios. With creative financing in your arsenal, you'll be better equipped to navigate the ever-changing real estate landscape and achieve your investment goals.

So, take that first step. Explore these creative financing options, and don't be afraid to think outside the box. Your next great real estate deal might just be waiting for a creative solution only you can provide.

BONUS CHAPTERS

Introduction to Real Estate Deal Analysis

Analyzing real estate deals can be a daunting task, but with the right tools and knowledge, it becomes much more manageable. One powerful tool we recommend is *The World's Greatest Real Estate Deal Analysis Spreadsheet*[TM]. This spreadsheet is designed to help you evaluate the financial viability of real estate investments with ease and precision.

In our book, *How to Analyze Real Estate Deals*, we delve deep into the intricacies of deal analysis, providing step-by-step instructions and expert insights. This introduction aims to give you a high-level overview of the process and how to effectively use the spreadsheet to make informed investment decisions.

The spreadsheet allows you to input various data points such as purchase price, mortgage details, monthly income, and annual expenses. It then performs complex calculations to provide you with key metrics like cash flow, return on investment (ROI), and internal rate of return (IRR).

By leveraging this tool, you can:

- Quickly assess the profitability of potential deals.
- Compare multiple investment opportunities.
- Make data-driven decisions to maximize your returns.

Whether you're a seasoned investor or just starting out, understanding how to analyze real estate deals is crucial for success.

Download Spreadsheet for Free

Unlock the full potential of your real estate investments by downloading *The World's Greatest Real Estate Deal Analysis Spreadsheet*™ for free.

Get your copy at: https://REFP.info/spreadsheet

We recommend always keeping an unedited, fresh copy on your hard drive in case you can't download the spreadsheet in the future.

Before analyzing a property, always make a new copy.

Spreadsheet Inputs

Entering the inputs into the spreadsheet is simple. Here's what you need to know:

- The manila fields indicate where you should input your data.
- The gray background with blue text shows the calculations that are automatically performed for you.

First, please name the deal that you're analyzing in the field just above the "Purchase Inputs". This will allow you to know which deal you're looking at if you're considering analyzing multiple deals or one deal multiple ways.

Purchase Inputs

Before we dive into the specifics of analyzing a real estate deal, let's go over the inputs required for the spreadsheet. These inputs will be divided into two columns: one for percentages and one for dollar amounts (or numbers).

Understanding what to enter in each field is crucial for accurately analyzing your deal. Let's go over what to put in each field next.

- **ARV** - Enter the After Repair Value, which is the estimated value of the property after all repairs and improvements have been made.
- **Purchase Price** - Enter the amount you are paying to acquire the property from the seller.
- **Seller Concessions** - Enter any financial concessions or incentives that the seller has agreed to provide, such as covering closing costs or offering repair credits.
- **Down Payment** - Enter the initial amount you will pay out-of-pocket towards the purchase of the property. Be sure to check out our guide on creative ways to come up with down payments for rental properties.
- **Closing Costs** - Enter the total costs associated with closing the real estate transaction, including title insurance, attorney fees, and other related expenses.
- **Rent Ready Costs** - Enter the expenses required to make the property ready for tenants, such as cleaning, repairs, and any necessary upgrades.
- **Cumulative Negative Cash Flow** - If you have negative cash flow enter the total cumulative amount of negative cash flow you anticipate before the property becomes cash flow positive. We recommend you set this aside to reduce risk. You may also want to check out our book on *How to Improve Cash Flow on Rental Properties* to get rid of negative cash flow on your properties.
- **Total Invested** - This is calculated for you. It is the cumulative amount of money you have invested in the

property, including **Down Payment**, **Closing Costs**, **Rent Ready Costs**, **Cumulative Negative Cash Flow**, minus any **Seller Concessions** you received from the seller.

Mortgage Inputs

To accurately analyze your real estate deal, it's essential to input detailed information about your mortgage and financing. These inputs will help calculate your monthly payments, interest costs, and overall financial commitment. Here's what you'll need to enter:

- **Mortgage Amount** - This is calculated for you. It is the total amount of money you are borrowing to finance the purchase of the property.
- **Mortgage Interest Rate** - Enter the annual interest rate for your mortgage. This is the percentage of the loan amount that you will pay as interest each year.
- **Loan Term** - Enter the duration of your mortgage loan in months. 360 months is a 30-year loan. This is the period over which you will repay the loan.
- **Private Mortgage Insurance** - Enter the monthly cost of private mortgage insurance (PMI) if applicable. PMI is typically required if your down payment is less than 20% of the purchase price. If you don't have PMI, use 0.000% here.
- **Drop PMI LTV** - Enter the loan-to-value (LTV) ratio at which PMI will be dropped. This is the point at which your equity in the property is high enough that PMI is no

longer required. If you don't have PMI, use 0.000% here.

Monthly Income

Accurately estimating your monthly income is critical for assessing the profitability of your real estate investment. This section will guide you through the necessary inputs for calculating your expected monthly income from the property, including rent and any additional sources of income.

- **Monthly Rent** - Enter the amount of rent you expect to receive from tenants each month. If you don't know how to determine what rent is on a property you're considering, you might want to check out our book on *How to Determine Rent Comps*.
- **Monthly Other Income** - Enter any additional monthly income from the property, such as parking fees, laundry services, or storage rentals.

Annual Expenses

Understanding and accurately estimating annual expenses is crucial for analyzing the financial viability of a real estate investment. This section will guide you through the various costs associated with owning and maintaining a property, from vacancy rates to property taxes and insurance. By thoroughly accounting for each of these expenses, you can better predict your investment's profitability and make more informed decisions.

- **Vacancy Rate** - Enter the percentage of time the property is expected to be vacant each year.
- **Property Taxes** - Enter the annual property tax amount you will pay for owning the property.
- **Property Insurance** - Enter the annual cost of insuring the property.
- **HOA Dues** - Enter the annual homeowner association fees, if applicable.
- **Utilities** - Enter the annual cost of utilities that you will pay as the property owner.
- **Other Expenses 1 and 2** - Enter any other annual expenses not covered in the previous categories.
- **Maintenance** - Enter the annual cost of maintaining the property, including repairs and routine upkeep.
- **CapEx** - Enter the annual amount set aside for capital expenditures. Consider our book and spreadsheet on CapEx for more guidance.
- **Management** - Enter the annual cost of property management services, if applicable.

Depreciation Details

Depreciation is a critical aspect of real estate investment analysis, as it allows you to account for the gradual reduction in the value of your property over time. Properly calculating and understanding depreciation can provide significant tax benefits and improve the overall financial picture of your investment. This section will guide you through the necessary inputs for determining depreciation, including land value, property type, and your effective income tax rate. By accurately inputting these details, you can optimize your investment strategy and maximize potential returns.

- **Land Value** - Enter the percent of the property that represents the value of the land. This value is used to calculate depreciation.
- **Property Type (C or R)** - Indicate whether the property is classified as commercial (C) or residential (R). This affects the depreciation schedule.
- **Effective Income Tax Rate** - Enter your effective income tax rate. This rate is used to estimate the tax benefits of depreciation.

Overrides

The spreadsheet is designed to be user-friendly on the Dashboard, while offering extensive functionality in the Overrides section. This dual approach ensures that users can easily navigate and input basic data, but also have access to more advanced features when needed.

In the Overrides tab, you have the ability to:

- **Modify any other inputs** - Adjust various parameters to suit your specific needs and scenarios.
- **Perform custom calculations** - Create and implement your own unique calculations to gain deeper insights into your investments.

- **View intermediate calculations** - Access detailed breakdowns of the calculations that drive the final results, providing transparency and better understanding.
- **Analyze performance over an extended period** - The spreadsheet allows you to conduct analysis through up to 40 years, enabling long-term strategic planning.
- **Track investment performance** - Use the Overrides tab to monitor how your investment evolves over time, making it easier to adjust your strategy as needed.

This comprehensive functionality ensures that the spreadsheet is not only a powerful tool for initial analysis but also a valuable resource for ongoing management and optimization of your real estate investments.

Dashboard

The Dashboard section provides a comprehensive overview of your real estate investment's key metrics and financial performance.

Here, you can quickly assess your monthly cash flow, return on investment (ROI), internal rate of return (IRR), and other critical indicators.

The Dashboard is designed to offer a user-friendly summary of your investment, allowing you to make informed decisions and track your progress over time.

Of course, you can dig into the Overrides tab for a ridiculous amount of additional detail.

Monthly Cash Flow - Year 1

This chart displays the Monthly Cash Flow, *Cash Flow from Depreciation*™, and the combined total, referred to as *True Cash Flow*™.

Understanding these metrics is crucial as they provide a comprehensive view of your investment's financial health.

- Monthly Cash Flow shows the actual cash inflow and outflow.
- *Cash Flow from Depreciation*™ accounts for tax benefits derived from property depreciation.
- *True Cash Flow*™ combines these figures, offering a more accurate representation of your investment's profitability.

Return in Dollars - Year 1

This chart displays the estimated dollars earned from your real estate investment over the first year, including Appreciation, Cash Flow, *Cash Flow from Depreciation*™, and Debt Paydown.

Understanding these metrics provides a holistic view of your investment's performance:

- **Appreciation** - Reflects the increase in property value over the year.
- **Cash Flow** - Shows the actual cash inflow and outflow.
- ***Cash Flow from Depreciation***™ - Accounts for tax benefits derived from property depreciation.

- **Debt Paydown** - Indicates the amount of principal paid down on your mortgage over the year.

Additionally, the chart includes earnings on reserves:

- **6 Months of Reserves in Savings** - Illustrates the interest earned if you set aside 6 months of reserves in a savings account.
- **Most of 12 Months of Reserves in Another Investment** - Shows the potential earnings if most of 12 months of reserves are invested in another investment vehicle like the stock market.

These combined figures provide a comprehensive representation of your investment's profitability and financial health over the first year.

You can see the totals at the bottom of the chart.

Return on Investment - Year 1

This chart displays the return on investment (ROI) from your real estate investment over the first year, including Appreciation, Cash Flow, *Cash Flow from Depreciation*™, and Debt Paydown.

Understanding these metrics provides a holistic view of your investment's performance:

- **Appreciation** - Reflects the increase in property value over the year divided by the total amount invested (and reserves where applicable).

- **Cash Flow** - Shows the actual cash inflow and outflow divided by the total amount invested (and reserves where applicable).
- *Cash Flow from Depreciation*™ - Accounts for tax benefits derived from property depreciation divided by the total amount invested (and reserves where applicable).
- **Debt Paydown** - Indicates the amount of principal paid down on your mortgage over the year divided by the total amount invested (and reserves where applicable).

Additionally, the chart includes ROI on reserves:

- **6 Months of Reserves in Savings** - Illustrates the interest earned if you set aside 6 months of reserves in a savings account, divided by the total amount invested plus 6 months of reserves.
- **Most of 12 Months of Reserves in Another Investment** - Shows the potential earnings if most of 12 months of reserves are invested in another investment vehicle like the stock market, divided by the total amount invested plus 12 months of reserves.

These combined figures provide a comprehensive representation of your investment's profitability and financial health over the first year in terms of ROI.

You can see the totals at the bottom of the chart.

Returns if Sold (ROI and IRR)

This chart illustrates the return on investment if you sold the property each year for the first 20 years. It includes three key metrics:

- **Simple Annualized Return on Investment** - This metric shows the average annual return on your investment, calculated by dividing the total return by the number of years you held the property.
- **Compound Annualized Return on Investment** - This metric accounts for the compounding effect, showing the average annual return on your investment when considering the reinvestment of earnings.
- **Internal Rate of Return (IRR)** - This metric represents the annualized rate of return that makes the net present value (NPV) of all cash flows (both inflows and outflows) from the investment equal to zero.

These metrics provide a comprehensive view of the financial performance of your investment over time, helping you to understand the potential long-term profitability and compare it with other investment opportunities.

Cash on Cash ROI & Cap Rate - Years 1-5

This chart displays the Cash on Cash Return on Investment (ROI) and the Capitalization Rate (Cap Rate) for the property over the first 5 years.

Understanding these metrics provides a comprehensive view of your investment's performance:

- **Cash on Cash ROI** - This metric shows the annual return on your investment based on the actual cash invested. It is calculated by dividing the annual pre-tax cash flow by the total cash invested.
- **Cap Rate** - This metric represents the annual return on the property based on its current market value. It is calculated by dividing the net operating income (NOI) by the property's current market value.

By understanding these metrics, you can gauge the effectiveness and profitability of your investment, enabling you to make well-informed decisions and evaluate it against other potential investment opportunities.

Return on True Net Equity™

This chart shows you the returns you're earning from Appreciation, Cash Flow, *Cash Flow from Depreciation*™, and Debt Paydown divided by the equity minus the costs to access that equity with a sale (what we call True Net Equity™). It shows the first 20 years. It also shows the total of all four areas of return.

Understanding these metrics is crucial for assessing the true profitability of your real estate investment:

- **Appreciation** - Reflects the increase in property value over the year.
- **Cash Flow** - Shows the actual cash inflow and outflow.

- ***Cash Flow from Depreciation*™** - Accounts for tax benefits derived from property depreciation.
- **Debt Paydown** - Indicates the amount of principal paid down on your mortgage over the year.

By dividing these returns by the True Net Equity™, you get a more accurate representation of your investment's performance, considering the costs to access the equity. This comprehensive view helps in making informed decisions and comparing the potential returns of different investments.

For more information on True Net Equity™ consider checking out our books about that:

- Should I Sell My Rental My Rental Property?
- Should I Sell My Refinance My Rental Property?

Annual Key Metrics - Year 1

This chart displays the financial performance of your real estate investment in terms of Gross Potential Income (GPI), Gross Operating Income (GOI), Operating Expenses (OpEx), and Net Operating Income (NOI) for the first year.

Understanding these metrics provides a comprehensive view of your investment's revenue and profitability:

- **Gross Potential Income (GPI)** - This metric represents the total income the property could generate if it were fully rented and all units were occupied at market rent rates, without accounting for any vacancies or losses.

- **Gross Operating Income (GOI)** - This metric reflects the actual income received from the property, including rent and other income sources, after accounting for vacancies and any collection losses.
- **Operating Expenses (OpEx)** - These are the costs associated with maintaining and managing the property, excluding mortgage payments and capital expenditures.
- **Net Operating Income (NOI)** - This metric is calculated by subtracting the operating expenses from the Gross Operating Income. It represents the income generated by the property after all operating expenses have been deducted.

By understanding these metrics, you can better assess the financial health and profitability of your real estate investment, helping you make more strategic decisions and compare it with other investment opportunities.

Annual Non-Loan Expenses - Year 1

This chart displays the financial performance of your real estate investment by itemizing all the non-loan expenses for the first year. Understanding these metrics provides a comprehensive view of your property's operational costs, which are crucial for accurate financial analysis and planning:

- **Vacancy Rate** - The percentage of time the property is expected to be vacant each year.
- **Property Taxes** - The annual amount paid for property taxes.

- **Property Insurance** - The cost of insuring the property for the year.
- **HOA Dues** - Annual homeowner association fees, if applicable.
- **Utilities** - The total annual cost of utilities paid by the property owner.
- **Other Expenses 1 and 2** - Any additional annual expenses not covered in the previous categories.
- **Maintenance** - The annual expense for maintaining the property, including routine repairs and upkeep.
- **CapEx** - The annual amount set aside for capital expenditures, such as major repairs or replacements.
- **Management Fees** - The cost of property management services, if utilized.

By breaking down these non-loan expenses, this chart helps you understand the total operational costs associated with your property, enabling you to better manage your investment and forecast its financial performance.

Equities and Cost-To-Access

This chart displays the equity in your real estate deal each year for the first 20 years, focusing on two key metrics: *True Net Equity*™ and Cash-Out Refi Equity.

- *True Net Equity*™ - This is the equity minus the costs to access it through a sale. It shows the real profit after considering selling costs.

104

- **Cash-Out Refi Equity** - This is the equity available if you refinance the property. It helps you understand the potential funds available through refinancing.
- **Cost-To-Access Equity Percentages** - The chart also shows the costs (as a percentage of the equity) associated with accessing each type of equity. This provides insight into the expenses involved.

Understanding these metrics is crucial for knowing how much money you could pull out of the investment over time and the cost to access that equity if you choose to do so.

94 Ways to Improve Cash Flow on Rental Properties

You might find yourself in a real estate market where:

- Property prices are high—possibly even soaring,
- Mortgage interest rates are elevated—maybe significantly so,
- Yet rents, despite any increases, haven't risen enough to offset these higher prices and rates.

Instead of the steady stream of cash flow you anticipated, you may be seeing just a trickle.

As a real estate broker, I developed the *Lowest Monthly Payment Guarantee*™ for my clients. This comprehensive checklist—backed by a *cash-in-your-pocket guarantee*—promised to uncover every possible way to reduce and minimize their monthly payments when purchasing a property.

For my real estate investor clients, I went a step further and created the *Maximum Cash Flow Guarantee*™. This second checklist—also backed by a *cash-in-your-pocket guarantee*—was designed to help them identify every possible way to increase and maximize the income generated from their rental properties.

Simply put, cash flow is the difference between income and expenses.

By maximizing income and minimizing expenses on a rental property, you can significantly boost your cash flow.

Below, you'll find an abridged version of these two checklists—combined into one—designed to help you maximize cash flow on your rental properties.

For your convenience, I've organized the strategies into seven distinct stages of the real estate investing process.

7 Distinct Real Estate Investing Stages for Improving Cash Flow

The real estate investing process can be broken down into seven distinct stages, each offering unique opportunities to improve cash flow:

1. **Searching for Properties** - Strategies to enhance cash flow while you're searching for a property to buy.

2. **Financing the Property** - Tactics to maximize cash flow when securing financing for the property you're purchasing.

3. **Improving the Real Estate Investing Strategy** - Different real estate investing strategies produce varying levels of cash flow. Here, you'll find strategies tailored to the specific investing approach you choose once you've acquired the property.

4. **Improving the Property** - Cash flow enhancement strategies based on making physical improvements to the property itself.

5. **Marketing the Property for Rent** - Techniques to boost cash flow during the process of marketing your property to prospective tenants.

6. **While Owning the Property** - Strategies you can implement at any time during ownership to optimize cash flow.

7. **While Renting the Property** - Methods to improve cash flow while actively renting out the property.

While applying strategies from each stage will maximize your cash flow, you can also focus on the stage you're currently in. Implement what you can now, and revisit these strategies regularly to continuously improve—aim for just a 1% improvement each month.

Searching for Properties

Here are the cash flow improving strategies to implement while searching for a property to buy.

- **Agent Selection** - Choosing the right real estate agent can have a significant impact on your investment's cash flow. Some agents offer lower commissions or commission rebates. This money can appear as improved cash flow in the first year or use the money to buy down your mortgage interest rate and get improved cash flow for the life of the loan.
- **Lock/Float** - When securing financing for a property, interest rates can fluctuate. Locking in an interest rate early can protect you from rising rates during the closing process, while floating allows you to benefit from potential rate drops. This decision can directly influence your cash flow by affecting your monthly mortgage payments. This is especially important when buying properties that have extended under contract periods like when buying new construction.
- **Search for Less Expensive Properties** - Lower-priced properties often come with smaller mortgage payments, which can improve cash flow if you're able to get the same rent as their more expensive alternatives. For every $10,000 less expensive the property, you save approximately $50 per month (when mortgage rates are in the 5% range). Some lower priced prices will have commensurately lower rents. Analyze each deal carefully to ensure that the overall income and expenses align to boost your cash flow.
- **Search for Pretty Properties** - Consider purchasing properties that are already in good condition and don't require significant fix-up costs. By doing so, you can allocate funds that would have been used for repairs to

increase your down payment or buy down the interest rate, both of which can lead to better cash flow.

- **Search for Seller Concessions** - Seller concessions are contributions from the seller to help cover your closing costs. By negotiating for these concessions, you can reduce your out-of-pocket expenses or even use them to buy down your mortgage interest rate, both of which enhance cash flow. Consider searching for properties that are offering seller concessions.
- **Search for Creative Financing** - Creative financing can offer more favorable terms than traditional loans, directly impacting your cash flow. Here are several types of creative financing to consider:

  - **Search for Owner Financing** - Owner financing involves the seller acting as the lender, which can lead to better terms than a traditional bank loan. This can reduce your monthly payments and improve cash flow. We define owner financing as when the seller does not have a mortgage; if they have a mortgage that's wrap financing or buying the property subject to their existing mortgage which we will cover next.
  - **Search for Wrap Financing** - In wrap financing, you agree to pay the seller a monthly amount that "wraps" around their existing mortgage. The seller keeps their original mortgage in place and continues making payments to their lender. You, in turn, make payments to the seller that cover both the existing mortgage and any additional amount you've agreed upon. This can result in a lower overall interest rate compared to obtaining new financing, which can

improve your cash flow. Wrap financing also gives the seller the protection of foreclosure rights if you fail to make payments.

- ○ **Search for Subject To**- In a "subject to" arrangement, you take ownership of the property while the seller's original mortgage stays in place. Instead of wrapping a new loan around the old one, you take over making payments directly to the lender on the seller's existing loan. The loan remains in the seller's name, but you're responsible for the payments. You're not formally accountable to the lender—it's not on your credit report—but you are responsible to the seller as per your agreement. This can be advantageous if the seller's mortgage has a lower interest rate than what's currently available. Like wrap financing, this can significantly reduce your mortgage expenses and boost cash flow. However, "subject to" financing typically doesn't offer the seller the same foreclosure protections as wrap financing does.

- ○ **Search for Assumable Loans** - Some loans can be formally transferred from the seller to the buyer, keeping the original interest rate intact. If the seller's loan has a lower interest rate, assuming the loan can significantly boost your cash flow. Since most loan assumptions are for owner-occupant borrowers this strategy likely only applies to those utilizing an owner-occupant investing strategy like house hacking or Nomad™.

- ○ **Search for Rent-To-Own Properties** - Rent-to-own agreements allow you to lease a property with the option to purchase it later. These arrangements can offer lower initial payments and more flexible terms, which may improve your cash flow compared to traditional financing.

- o **Search for Agreements for Deed** - Also called bond for deed, contract for deed, or installment land contracts, these arrangements let you pay the seller directly over time. You get the deed after fulfilling the contract. This can lead to lower payments and improved cash flow while you're repaying.
- o **Search for Seller Financing** - Seller financing typically involves the seller offering a loan to cover a portion of the purchase price, often as a second mortgage or "carryback" loan. In this scenario, you would secure the primary mortgage from a traditional lender, and the seller finances the remaining balance. For example, if you purchase a property for $200,000, you might get a $160,000 loan from a bank, with the seller providing a $40,000 loan. This setup can result in more favorable terms, such as lower interest rates or flexible payment schedules, improving your overall cash flow. Unlike owner financing, where the seller finances the entire purchase, seller financing usually complements other financing sources, reducing the need for a larger bank loan.

Once you've found a promising property using the strategies above, the next step is to optimize your financing to further enhance your cash flow. Let's explore the various ways you can improve your cash flow during the financing stage of your real estate investment.

Financing the Property

Here are the cash flow improving strategies to implement while financing the property you're buying.

Before Getting Loan

Here are a few strategies to improve cash flow to use before getting your loan.

- **Lender Selection** - Shop around for lenders to find one that offers better interest rates, lower fees, or more favorable terms. Different lenders have varying costs and requirements, so comparing multiple options on the same day can ensure you get the best deal, improving your overall cash flow.
- **Select by Closing Costs** - Some loans come with higher closing costs than others. By selecting a loan with lower closing costs, especially if you plan to finance these costs, you can reduce the amount you need to borrow, leading to better cash flow due to lower monthly payments.
- **Lock/Float** - Decide whether to lock in your interest rate early to protect against potential rate increases before closing, or to float and take advantage of possible rate decreases. Locking your rate provides security, while floating offers flexibility, both of which can impact your cash flow depending on market conditions.

- **Offer Less** - Negotiating a lower purchase price directly reduces the amount you need to finance, leading to lower monthly mortgage payments. This strategy can also leave more of your resources available for other cash flow improvement tactics.

Pay Upfront Instead of Financing

Here are some strategies for improving cash flow that deal with opting to pay fees upfront instead of financing them.

- **Seller Concessions** - Negotiate for the seller to cover some of your closing costs or to provide credits that can be used to buy down your mortgage interest rate. This is almost certainly required to be done at the time you make your offer and not after your offer is accepted. This reduces your upfront cash outlay and can lower your monthly mortgage payments, thereby improving cash flow.
- **Pay Closing Costs** - Paying your closing costs upfront instead of rolling them into your mortgage can reduce the amount you borrow, lowering your monthly payments and improving cash flow over the life of the loan.
- **Pre-Pay PMI** - If you're required to pay Private Mortgage Insurance (PMI), consider pre-paying it in a lump sum rather than monthly. This reduces your ongoing monthly expenses, leading to better cash flow.
- **Staggered Rate** - Opt for a staggered interest rate loan, where the interest rate is lower in the initial years

and increases over time. This can provide you with better cash flow during the early years of the loan when you may need it most.

- **Buy Down Rate** - Pay upfront to lower your mortgage interest rate for the life of the loan. A lower interest rate means a lower monthly payment, which can significantly improve your cash flow over time. For long-term buy and hold real estate investors—especially if you find yourself in a low mortgage interest rate environment— this can be an amazing strategy.

Change/Improve Borrower(s)

These strategies for improving cash flow relate to changing or improving the borrower on the loan.

- **Credit Score** - Improving your credit score can help you secure a lower interest rate and reduce your PMI rate. Both of these improvements lead to lower monthly payments and better cash flow.
- **Add Borrower** - Adding a co-borrower with a strong credit profile to your loan can help you qualify for a better interest rate and lower PMI, both of which can enhance your cash flow.
- **Remove Borrower** - If one borrower has a weaker credit profile, removing them from the loan might result in a better interest rate. This can lead to lower monthly payments and improved cash flow.
- **Loan Partner** - Partnering with someone who has a strong financial profile can help you secure better loan

terms, including lower interest rates and more favorable conditions, which ultimately enhance your cash flow.

Relationship With Lender

These cash flow improving strategies are based on your relationship with the lender or lending institution.

- **Auto Pay Loan** - Setting up automatic payments can sometimes qualify you for a slight reduction in your interest rate, directly improving your cash flow by lowering your monthly mortgage payment. It may show up also as a penalty to the interest rate if you don't use autopay for the mortgage.
- **Additional Accounts** - Maintaining additional accounts or depositing more funds with your lender might earn you a small interest rate reduction, leading to improved cash flow through lower monthly payments. This is more common with commercial loans and relationship banking.

Change Amortization

These strategies to improve your cash flow deal with changing the amortization schedule of the financing you're getting.

- **Interest Only** - An interest-only loan allows you to pay only the interest for a certain period, which significantly reduces your monthly payments. This can boost your cash flow in the short term, though it comes with long-term risks since the principal remains unpaid. You'll need to have a solid plan to deal with the loan balance when the ballon payment date arrives.

- **Negative Amortization** - A negative amortizing loan allows you to pay less than the interest due, causing the loan balance to increase over time. This lowers your initial payments and improves short-term cash flow but increases your debt over time.
- **Rate from Loan Term** - Shortening the loan term (e.g., switching from a 30-year to a 15-year mortgage) can lower your interest rate. However, this typically increases your monthly payments, so it's more about long-term savings than immediate cash flow improvement.
- **Loan Term** - Extending the loan term (e.g., from 30 to 40 years) reduces the monthly payment amount, which can improve your cash flow. However, this means you'll pay more interest over the life of the loan.

Loan Terms

These cash flow improving strategies deal with the terms (details) of the loan itself.

- **Amount Borrowed** - Putting more money down reduces the amount you need to borrow, leading to lower monthly payments. This can improve your cash flow, though it also means tying up more capital in the property.

- **Loan-To-Value** - A lower loan-to-value (LTV) ratio, achieved by making a larger down payment, often results in a better interest rate. This lowers your monthly payments and improves cash flow. Not only can putting more down improve your LTV and give you a better interest rate, but it might also reduce your Private Mortgage Insurance (PMI) payment since that's part of the calculation for determining PMI amounts.
- **Adjustable Rate** - An adjustable-rate mortgage (ARM) typically starts with a lower interest rate than a fixed-rate mortgage. This can enhance your cash flow in the initial years, though the rate—and your payments—can increase later.

Private Mortgage Insurance (PMI)

These strategies to improve cash flow deal primarily with Private Mortgage Insurance (PMI).

What is PMI? The lender would prefer you put at least 20% down to finance a property. With 20% down they feel comfortable enough that if you don't pay as agreed they will be able to foreclose, sell the property and get all their money back after the expenses of foreclosure and sale.

You insist on putting less than 20% down.

They may reluctantly agree, but they may charge you a higher interest rate because it is a riskier loan to them. And, additionally, they may insist that you pay a third-party insurance company a fee that insures them in case you default and they're unable to foreclose and sell the property to recoup their entire investment. This third-party insurance company is Private Mortgage Insurance.

It is insurance you pay for to protect the lender in case you default on the loan.

- **Eliminate PMI** - If you can put down at least 20% of the purchase price, you can avoid PMI altogether, significantly reducing your monthly mortgage expenses and improving your cash flow.
- **Pre-Pay PMI** - Paying PMI in a lump sum upfront instead of monthly can reduce your ongoing costs, leading to better cash flow throughout the loan term.
- **Improve Credit** - Enhancing your credit score can help you secure a lower PMI rate or even eliminate PMI altogether if your LTV ratio improves, both of which contribute to better cash flow.
- **Add Borrowers** - Added a borrower to your loan typically reduces PMI and therefore improves cash flow.

Other Properties

These cash flow improving strategies rely on tapping into other properties you own.

Some of these strategies deal with making sure your cash flow is optimized for your entire portfolio (including these other properties) and not specifically to a new property you're buying.

- **Cash Out Refi to Buy/Refi** - Consider doing a cash-out refinance on another property to use the proceeds for purchasing or refinancing your current property. This can result in better overall financing terms and improved cash flow.
- **Cash Out Refi for Larger Down Payment** - If putting more down on your current property will secure a better interest rate or eliminate PMI, consider using funds from a cash-out refinance on another property. This can lower your monthly payments and improve cash flow.
- **Rate and Term Before Acquisition** - Before purchasing a new property, consider refinancing your existing properties to better terms. As you own more properties the complexity of refinancing increases significantly. Consider this a reminder to consider this before each new purchase and to make any changes to other properties now before you add a new property that further limits what you can do. This can also improve the overall cash flow on your portfolio and might also allow you to qualify for better financing on the new purchase.

Non-Traditional Financing

These are some non-traditional financing strategies for improving cash flow you might want to consider.

- **Pay Cash** - If you have sufficient funds, paying cash for a property eliminates the need for financing altogether, which maximizes cash flow by removing monthly mortgage payments.

- **Private Financing** - Secure a loan from family or friends (private lenders) who might offer more favorable terms than traditional banks. This can lead to lower monthly payments and improved cash flow.
- **Creative Financing** - Explore options like owner financing, wrap financing, agreement for deed, lease-options, or subject to, where the seller might offer better terms than traditional lenders. These strategies can lower your mortgage payments and enhance cash flow.
- **Assumable Loan** - If the seller's existing loan has a lower interest rate than current market rates, assuming their loan can be a great way to secure better financing terms, leading to improved cash flow. This is more likely for owner-occupant loans, so this is probably limited to owner-occupant investing strategies like house hacking or Nomad™.

While optimizing your financing is crucial for improving cash flow, it's equally important to consider how your chosen real estate investing strategy can impact your returns. Let's now explore various strategies that can enhance your cash flow by refining your overall investment approach.

Improving the Real Estate Investing Strategy

Here are the cash flow improving strategies based on improving the real estate investing strategy you're opting to utilize.

- **Term** - Adjusting the duration of your lease can significantly impact your cash flow. Shorter-term rentals, such as daily, weekly, or monthly leases, often command higher rents compared to yearly leases. However, shorter terms can also lead to increased expenses, including higher vacancy rates, more frequent marketing, and potentially higher management and maintenance costs. Offering different terms, such as furnished vs. unfurnished rentals, can also cater to various market segments, like vacation rentals or boarding houses, providing opportunities to maximize income.

- **Lease-Option** - Lease-option strategies, including variations like rent-to-own (like lease-purchases and lease-options), can dramatically improve cash flow, particularly in markets where buying is significantly more expensive than renting. These arrangements typically involve collecting a non-refundable purchase deposit/option fee, which can—mathematically—appear to add hundreds of dollars per month to your cash flow. Additionally, tenants in lease-option agreements often treat the property with more care, reducing maintenance, vacancy, and management costs. This strategy is a form of our *Deal Alchemy*™, where you trade future appreciation returns for immediate cash flow.

- **Niche** - Specializing in a specific rental market can allow you to charge premium rents by catering to unique needs. For example, you might focus on corporate rentals, traveling nurses, or student housing. By understanding and addressing the specific requirements of your niche audience, such as providing furnished units for corporate rentals or flexible leases for students, you can add value that justifies higher rental rates. The key is to determine what additional services or amenities you can offer that will attract your target market and what premium you can reasonably charge for those services.

The following cash flow improving strategies are really just variations of house hacking where you're renting out part of the property you're living in for income and to improve cash flow. However, you could utilize these strategies even when you're not living in the property.

- **Roommates** - Renting out individual bedrooms in a single-family home, or additional units in a duplex, triplex, or fourplex, can significantly increase your cash flow. This is a common house hacking strategy where you live in one part of the property and rent out the rest. For example, you might rent out spare bedrooms in your own home or lease the other units in a multi-family property. This approach allows you to maximize the rental income from a single property by utilizing every available space.

- **Rent by Bed/Bedroom** - Some properties, particularly those near colleges or universities, may lend themselves well to renting by the bedroom or even by the bed. This strategy works particularly well with student housing, where multiple tenants share a single property. By renting out each bedroom or bed individually, you can often achieve a higher overall rent compared to leasing the entire property to a single tenant.

- **Rent by Parts** - Renting out different parts of a property, such as non-conforming units in a duplex, triplex, or fourplex, can be a lucrative strategy. It's essential to check local occupancy laws to ensure compliance. This strategy can also include more unconventional setups, such as renting out RV parking spaces, tiny homes, garages, or storage units on the property. These spaces don't have to be residential; they can be rented for commercial or recreational purposes, such as storage or use of shared community amenities like a pool or recreational center.

While optimizing your real estate investing strategy can significantly boost cash flow, another powerful approach is to enhance the property itself. By making strategic improvements and modifications to your rental property, you can potentially increase its value and appeal, leading to higher rental income and improved cash flow. Let's explore some effective strategies for improving cash flow through property enhancements.

Improving the Property

Here are the cash flow improving strategies based on making improvements to the property.

- **Subdivide** - Consider subdividing your property into multiple units to increase rental income. For example, you could rent the upstairs and downstairs separately, offering tenants more privacy while still sharing common areas like heating, cooling, mail, laundry, and possibly even the kitchen or living areas. This isn't the same as converting the property into a formal duplex or triplex; instead, it's more about creating a roommate-like situation with more separation. This setup allows you to comply with local roommate laws and zoning requirements while potentially charging higher rents, as tenants may feel like they have their own space.
- **Upgrade Property** - Enhancing your property's curb appeal and overall condition can justify charging higher rents. Improvements could include landscaping, painting, adding or improving shutters, lawn care, updating the mailbox, property address numbers, or exterior lighting. These upgrades can attract higher-paying tenants and increase the property's value. This approach is also common in value-add strategies or the BRRRR method, where the goal is to improve the property to increase its rent and overall profitability.
- **Solar** - Installing solar panels and including the cost of electricity in the base rent can make your property more attractive to tenants who value energy efficiency, potentially allowing you to charge higher rents.

However, you should be cautious about the legal implications of charging for utilities, as this can sometimes enter a gray area. It's advisable to consult with a local attorney to ensure compliance with utility billing regulations.

- **Furnished Rental** - Offering a furnished rental can significantly increase the rent you can charge, especially if you shift your strategy to short-term or medium-term rentals, such as vacation rentals, student rentals, or corporate housing. Furnished rentals appeal to tenants looking for convenience and are often willing to pay a premium for a move-in ready home.
- **Convert Property** - Converting a single-family property into a duplex, triplex, or fourplex can increase your rental income by creating multiple rental units within the same property. This approach is especially effective if the property is already somewhat set up for such a conversion. However, it may be cost-prohibitive or even impossible if significant structural changes are required or if zoning laws restrict such conversions. Always check with your city and county regarding zoning and licensing requirements before starting any conversion work, as this can also affect the types of loans you can secure and their terms, including the loan-to-value ratio.
- **Improvement Rent** - Charging extra rent for specific property improvements can help offset the cost of upgrades while increasing your overall rental income. For example, you might charge a tenant more for installing new carpet or a fence. While you may not be able to recoup the full cost of the improvement from a single tenant, some upgrades, like a fence, can justify

higher rents with future tenants as well, allowing you to gradually recover your investment and potentially earn a return. This strategy is particularly useful for items with a long lifespan, where the cost can be spread out over multiple tenancies.

While property improvements can significantly boost your rental income, the way you market your property can be equally important for maximizing cash flow. By implementing effective marketing strategies, you can attract high-quality tenants, reduce vacancy periods, and potentially command higher rents. Let's explore some key strategies for improving cash flow through smart marketing techniques.

Marketing the Property for Rent

Here are the cash flow improving strategies to implement while you're marketing your property for rent.

- **Optimize Marketing** - Effective marketing starts with high-quality materials. Ensure that you have professional-grade photos, a 3D tour, and a video to showcase your property. These elements can significantly enhance the appeal of your listing, attracting more potential tenants. Additionally, use online marketing as well as flyers and signs strategically around the neighborhood to increase visibility. Well-designed marketing materials make your property stand out and convey a sense of professionalism that can justify higher rent and reduce vacancy periods.

- **Maximize Exposure** - To attract the right tenants, it's crucial to advertise your property across all available platforms where tenants might be searching. This includes online rental websites, social media, and community bulletin boards. Physical advertising, such as yard signs and directional signs leading to the property, can also capture the attention of local renters. By maximizing exposure, you increase the chances of filling vacancies quickly and with quality tenants.

- **Sales Skills** - Mastering sales skills is essential for renting your property at the highest possible rate and minimizing vacancy. This includes both phone skills for initial inquiries and in-person salesmanship during property tours. Being persuasive and knowledgeable helps you connect with potential tenants, address their concerns, and highlight the property's best features, ultimately leading to faster lease agreements and better tenant retention.

- **Optimize Showings** - Preparing your property for showings is a key step in securing a lease. Ensure the property is well-lit, smells pleasant, and is clean, neat, and in good repair. First impressions matter, and a well-presented property can make the difference between a potential tenant choosing your property over another. Additionally, create a sense of scarcity by scheduling back-to-back showings and mentioning this when booking appointments. This strategy can create urgency and increase interest among prospective tenants.

While effective marketing strategies can help attract tenants and maximize rental income, it's equally important to focus on optimizing your property's financial performance during ownership. Let's explore various strategies you can implement to improve cash flow throughout your tenure as a property owner.

While Owning the Property

Here are the cash flow improving strategies to implement while you own the property.

Refi/Pay Off Loan

Managing your mortgage can be one of the most effective ways to improve cash flow and overall property profitability.

- **Refi to Extend Term** - If your loan is old enough, consider refinancing to extend the loan term. This can lower your monthly payments and—if interest rates have dropped and/or your loan-to-value has improved—potentially secure a better interest rate, improving your cash flow.
- **Refi to Improve Rate** - If interest rates have dropped since you first took out your mortgage, refinancing to a lower rate can reduce your monthly payments and save you money over the life of the loan.
- **Payoff Loan** - If you have the financial means, paying off your loan in its entirety can eliminate your mortgage payments, drastically improving your monthly cash flow and reducing financial stress.

Taxes

Property taxes are a significant expense for any property owner, and managing them effectively can save you money.

- **Correct Assessor** - Ensure that the county assessor has accurate information about your property's condition and characteristics. Correcting any inaccuracies can prevent overvaluation and keep your taxes in check.
- **Contest Tax Increases** - If your property taxes increase, consider contesting the increase. Successful challenges can lead to reduced tax bills and improved cash flow.
- **Vote** - Participate in local elections and vote on measures that affect property taxes. Being informed and voting appropriately can help control future tax increases.

Insurance

Insurance is essential for protecting your investment, but it's also an area where you can manage costs.

- **Shop Insurance Rates** - Regularly compare insurance rates from different providers to ensure you're getting the best deal. Competitive rates can lower your insurance costs without sacrificing coverage.
- **Insurance Coverage** - Review your property insurance policy to make sure you have the right level of coverage. Avoid overpaying for unnecessary coverage or underinsuring your property. It is not just about

minimizing this cost while sacrificing coverage; you must make sure you minimize cost while keeping a desirable level of coverage. Sacrificing coverage is short-sighted and might significantly hurt cash flow if you ever have a claim that is you opted not to cover.

- **Insured** - Adjust your insurance policy by adding or removing people as needed to optimize your rates. This can lead to lower premiums.
- **Insurance Deductible** - Consider raising your deductible to lower your insurance premium. Taking on more risk personally can reduce your monthly insurance costs. See comments about sacrificing coverage being short-sighted above.
- **Remove PMI** - Totally different type of insurance, but if your property's equity has increased sufficiently, you may be able to remove Private Mortgage Insurance (PMI). This can significantly reduce your monthly mortgage payment.

Making Payments

How you manage your payments can also impact your overall costs.

- **Discount for Autopay** - Sign up for autopay on utilities and other bills to avoid per-bill fees. Many service providers offer small discounts or waive fees for customers who enroll in autopay.
- **Discount for Early Payments** - Some service providers, such as HOA or insurance companies, offer

discounts for early payments. Paying these bills in advance can reduce your overall expenses.

Management

Whether you manage your property yourself or hire a professional, effective management is key to maintaining profitability.

- **Self-Manage** - If you choose to manage the property yourself, ensure you stay up to date with the latest laws, best practices, and compliance issues. Self-management can save on property management fees, but it often requires a significant time investment.
- **Professional Property Manager** - Shop around for a high-quality property manager who offers reasonable fees. A good property manager can maximize your rental income and minimize headaches.
- **Manage the Manager** - Even with a professional property manager, it's important to regularly review management statements for accuracy. Mistakes can happen, and catching them early can save you money.
- **Insist on Best Practices** - Ensure your property manager follows best practices, such as marketing your property early and raising rents with each lease renewal. This proactive approach can help maximize your rental income.

Maintenance

Regular maintenance is crucial for keeping your property in good condition and minimizing vacancies.

- **Maintain Property** - Regularly maintaining your property can reduce the time it spends vacant between tenants. A well-maintained property attracts tenants quickly and reduces downtime.
- **Quality Materials** - Using quality materials for maintenance and repairs may have a higher upfront cost, but it can lower the overall cost of maintenance over time by reducing the frequency of repairs and replacements.

Depreciation

Depreciation can provide significant tax benefits, and managing it strategically can enhance your investment returns.

- **Accelerate Depreciation** - Consider accelerating depreciation on your property to maximize tax benefits in the short term. This strategy can improve your cash flow by reducing your taxable income, but it should be used with careful planning to avoid potential future tax liabilities. This can be one of the larger improvements to your cash flow.

While the strategies for improving cash flow during property ownership are crucial, it's equally important to optimize your rental income while renting it. Let's explore various techniques you can implement to enhance your cash flow during the rental phase of your investment.

While Renting the Property

Here are the cash flow improving strategies to implement while you're renting the property.

Add Services

Offering additional services can increase rental income and enhance tenant satisfaction.

- **Additional Services** - Consider offering additional services such as high-speed internet, cable, or utilities for an extra fee. Tenants often value the convenience of bundled services, making this an effective way to boost your rental income. However, be sure to check local laws, as this practice may not be permitted in some areas.
- **DFY Services** - Offer done-for-you (DFY) services such as lawn care, snow removal, or house cleaning. These services can be billed as extras, appealing to tenants who prefer convenience and are willing to pay for it.

Charge Appropriately

Setting appropriate charges can maximize your rental income while offering flexibility to tenants.

- **Bill Back** - Implement bill-back strategies for utilities or HOA services, such as charging tenants for non-potable water or other shared resources. This helps to ensure that tenants are covering their fair share of costs, improving your net income.
- **Tier Rent by Credit Score** - Adjust rent based on the tenant's credit score, with higher rent for those with lower scores. This can also apply to security deposits, where tenants with better credit pay less upfront. Check with your attorney before implementing this strategy.
- **Pet Rent** - Charge additional rent for tenants with pets. Pet rent can help cover potential wear and tear caused by pets and increase your overall rental income.

Convenience Billing

Convenience billing options can make it easier for tenants to pay rent while potentially increasing your revenue.

- **Billing Frequency** - Offer more frequent billing options, such as weekly or biweekly payments, instead of the traditional monthly schedule. This can be attractive to tenants who prefer smaller, more manageable payments but can also produce more cash flow over the same period.
- **Autopay** - Here are conflicting ideas where both options may ultimately improve cash flow. Encourage tenants to enroll in autopay by offering a discount or, conversely, charge a fee for those who do not use autopay. Autopay

can reduce late payments and ensure consistent cash flow.

- **Discount On-Time Payment** - Provide a discount for tenants who pay their rent on time or early, incentivizing prompt payments and reducing the need for late payment penalties.
- **Term** - Adjust the term of rental agreements to fit different rental strategies. Consider offering daily, weekly, or short-term/vacation rentals, which can often command higher rents than traditional monthly leases.

Timing

Optimizing the timing of lease agreements and renewals can minimize vacancies and maximize rental income.

- **Notice** - Require a 60-90 day notice from tenants if they intend not to renew their lease. This provides you with ample time to market the property and secure a new tenant, reducing vacancy periods.
- **Start Early/Test Rent** - Begin marketing the property early, even before the current tenant moves out, and start with a higher rent to test the market. This strategy allows you to adjust pricing based on demand and secure the best possible rental rate.
- **Renew Peak Season** - Align lease renewal dates to end during peak rental seasons, such as spring or summer, when demand is higher. This increases the likelihood of filling the property quickly and possibly at a higher rent.

Miscellaneous

Implementing additional requirements can protect your property and reduce potential liabilities.

- **Renter's Insurance** - Require tenants to carry renter's insurance. This protects both you and the tenant in case of damage to the property or loss of personal belongings, reducing potential conflicts and liabilities.

Conclusion

This guide has explored 94 ways to improve cash flow on rental properties across seven distinct stages of your real estate investing process.

Each stage presents unique opportunities to boost your investment's financial performance, and the cumulative effect of applying these strategies can significantly increase your property's profitability.

By focusing on cash flow improvement at every stage, you can:

- Build a more resilient and profitable real estate portfolio
- Enhance property values—especially for properties where value is driven by the income they generate, such as commercial properties
- Strengthen your ability to secure favorable financing by improving loan-to-value (LTV) and debt service coverage ratios
- Optimize tax benefits

- Accelerate savings for larger down payments and quickly replenish reserves
- Increase tenant satisfaction by enhancing the tenant experience, improving retention rates, and reducing turnover costs

Remember, even small adjustments across multiple areas can compound into substantial gains in your overall returns and financial stability.

Make it a habit to regularly review and implement these strategies, tailoring them to fit your specific properties and market conditions.

With consistent effort and strategic application, you can transform your rental properties into powerful, cash-generating assets that support your long-term financial goals.

Introduction to Monte Carlo Analysis of Rental Properties

There's a problem with how we've been modeling our investments so far. It is not unique to us. Almost everyone does it wrong.

But, we're going to fix it now.

The issue is the assumptions we've been using and how the real world works.

For the analysis we've been doing with *The World's Greatest Real Estate Deal Analysis Spreadsheet*™ (TWGREDAS)—and any other real estate deal analysis spreadsheet—we've used static assumptions.

We might assume that property values are going up by 3% per year. Well, that's not truly a correct representation of reality.

Heck, with the overrides tab in TWGREDAS we may have said, they go up by 3% for the first 3 years and then only 2% thereafter. Better, but still not reality.

The truth is: we really don't know how much property values will go up as we hold the property. They could go up by 3%. They could go down by 3%. They could go up then down or down then up. Could be more or less than 3%. Might be 3.1% or 2.9%. Might be up or down 6% or 10%.

If we look back at history (and we do when we consider the risks of investing in real estate), we can see what property appreciation has done over the last 100 years.

Risk Matrix: Appreciation

Likelihood	Severity				
	0 Increase	1 Small Decline	2 Medium Decline	3 Large Decline	4 Catastrophic
1	>10% Increase 7.7%			10-15% Decline 6.0%	>15% Decline 0.0%
2	5-10% Increase 15.0%		5-10% Decline 12.8%		
3	0-5% Increase 25.6%	0-5% Decline 34.6%			

So, to correctly model how our investment might perform, we should not use a static 3% per year—or whatever static number you believe to be true—for property appreciation.

Our crystal balls are broken. We can't accurately predict—exactly—what appreciation will be for our properties.

We can guess. Based on what has happened in the past they will average about 3% per year.

But they may:

- Increase in value by more than 10% for the year about 7.7% of the time
- Increase between 5% and 10% for the year about 15% of the time
- Increase between 0% and 5% for the year about 25.6% of the time
- Go down in value between 0% and 5% for the year about 34.6% of the time

- Go down in value between 5% and 10% for the year about 12.8% of the time
- Go down in value between 10% and 15% for the year about 6% of the time

These are based on what has happened over the last 100 years. Could the future be different? Absolutely.

But it is much more accurate than just assuming that they will be going up in value by 3% per year every year.

Not Just Property Appreciation

As you probably guessed, this isn't just an issue with property appreciation. It applies to other assumptions we have as well.

Here's a list of some of the more significant ones:

- **Property Appreciation Rate** - This is the one we've been talking about already. It is how much properties go up or down in value.
- **Rent Appreciation Rate** - This is how much rents increase or decrease with each lease renewal.
- **Inflation Rate** - Inflation reflects the overall increase in prices and the decrease in purchasing power over time. It impacts everything from the cost of goods and services to the value of money itself. In the context of your portfolio, inflation affects how much your money will be worth in the future, influencing the real returns on your investments. For instance, even if your rental

income and property values rise, high inflation could erode those gains in terms of actual purchasing power. A million dollars today isn't the same as a million dollars 50 years ago and it won't be the same as a million dollars 50 years from now.

- **Mortgage Interest Rates - Mortgage Interest Rates** - Mortgage rates fluctuate over time. The rate you secure for your current property purchase or refinance won't necessarily be the same for properties you buy in one, five, or more years from now.
- **Stock Market Rate of Return** - This is how much you're earning on money you have invested in the stock market. This also applies to other investments you might have like savings accounts, bonds, CDs, cryptocurrencies, etc.

If you really want to go to freaky town, you could also model this with changing tax rates, insurance rates, maintenance and capital expenses on the property.

Does This Even Matter?

Does this even matter and why should I care?

Let's start with a simple example of someone who invests in stocks. They don't even buy a home to live in; they rent instead.

They invest approximately 10% of their income in the stock market earning 8% per year.

Using static assumptions, we could calculate that they would be financially independent (FI) after about 53.25 years.

See **Error! Reference source not found.** at the end of the chapter. We moved the charts to the end of the chapter—instead of inline—so we could show you larger, readable versions of the charts.

But what if we used a reasonable range of values for the return from the stock market instead of always 8% every year?

We could use a range of values that better approximates what the stock markets has done historically—still averaging about 8% for this selection of stocks.

Instead of seeing a smooth line showing their journey toward financial independence as shown in Error! Reference source not found. at the end of the chapter.

We'd instead see a less smooth line representing how the stock market returns change each month like Error! Reference source not found..

And, if we ran it 10 times, you'd see that when they actually achieve financial independence (when the line crosses the horizontal dotted line) is a little different each time. See Error! Reference source not found..

If the stock market performs well, they're financially independent earlier. If the stock market does not perform as well, they end up being financially independent later.

If we ran this 1,000 times and summarized the results, we can see the range of when they're financially independent. See Error! Reference source not found..

Monte Carlo Modeling

This type of analysis is called Monte Carlo modeling.

Monte Carlo modeling is a statistical technique used to simulate multiple potential outcomes for an investment or financial scenario.

It works by:

- Running hundreds or thousands of simulations with varying input parameters
- Analyzing the range and probability of different outcomes
- Providing a more nuanced understanding of potential risks and returns

For real estate investing, Monte Carlo analysis involves varying input factors such as property appreciation rates, rent increases, mortgage interest rates, inflation, and market returns. This approach allows you to better assess the likelihood of achieving your financial goals and understand the potential risks associated with your investment strategies.

I like to call it *Alternate Universe Modeling*™ because we're consider how your investments might perform if you were living in alternate universes with different futures.

Back to our example with someone just investing in stocks.

In Error! Reference source not found. at the end of the chapter:

- The light blue band shows the full range of results from the very worst to the very best.
- The darker blue band in the middle shows you the middle 50% of all runs. Half of the time the results are this darker band.
- The dark link at the very center shows you the median value. Half the values are higher than this. Half the values are lower than this.

If we look at the median line we can see that half the time they're financially independent around 58 years. Half the time it is after 58 years.

It could have been as early as year 48. And, it could take longer than 60 years—when we stopped modeling for this example. In fact, only about 85% of the 1,000 runs we ran were financially independent 60 years from when they started.

We can summarize this is a different chart and show what percentage of the 1,000 runs were financially independent in each month. That's Error! Reference source not found..

By using a range of values for things like the stock market rate of return, we get a much more nuanced understanding of what is likely to happen.

What If They Became Homeowners Instead of Renting?

Our last example they were renting a property to live in and investing in stocks.

What if they bought on owner-occupant property with 5% down to live in and invested in stocks?

If we used static assumptions they would be financially independent about 15 and half years faster as shown in Error! Reference source not found. at the end of the chapter.

Part of what gets them to financial independence faster is that they end up paying off their owner-occupant property 30 years after they buy it. Without a mortgage payment the threshold for them being financially independent is a little lower.

There's a little more to this story, but I don't want to go off into the weeds here. The punchline is they achieve financial independence faster with static assumptions as you can see in Error! Reference source not found..

Let's vary the property appreciation rate, mortgage interest rate, inflation rate, and stock market rate of return. If we were discussing rentals, we'd vary the rent appreciation rate as well but in this case they're not buying any rentals; we'll get to that shortly.

With variable property appreciation rates, mortgage interest rates until they lock in a 30-year fixed rate financing loan, inflation rate and stock market rate of return it looks like Error! Reference source not found..

They're financially independent as early as 33.75 years from when they start. In 99.5% of the 1,000 runs they're financially independent by the time we stop modeling at 60 years.

How does this compare to them just investing in stocks? Let's show both on one chart in Error! Reference source not found..

Buying an owner-occupant property seems to make a pretty big difference.

If we just look at what percentage of the 1,000 runs they achieve financial independence, you can see that buying the owner-occupant property is more probable (higher percentage of the runs achieve it) and they're financially independent earlier (it happens more to the left on the chart). See Error! Reference source not found..

Buying Rental Properties with 20% Down Payments

Let's assume, for now, that they don't buy an owner-occupant property with 5% down. Instead, they decide to buy 20% down rental properties as their primary investing strategy.

Any additional money beyond what they need for the rentals is still investing in stocks, but whenever they get enough for a 20% down payment they buy a rental property with very modest cash flow.

They're willing to buy up to ten 20% down payment rentals.

If we have **static assumptions** for property appreciation, rent appreciation, inflation, mortgage interest rates and the stock market rate of return, they might be financially independent after 31 years.

With static assumptions, that's about 18.67 years faster than just investing in stocks and about 3 years faster than buying an owner-occupant property and investing stocks as shown in Error! Reference source not found..

With static assumptions, they achieve financial independence faster. See Error! Reference source not found..

And, still looking at the chart above, they appear have a lot more income coming then just investing in stocks the longer they hold the rental properties.

In fact, they're earning about twice what they need to be financially independent about 48.5 years in. That means they're earning twice what they need to be financially independent before just investing in stocks as a renter is even earning enough for them to financially independent at all.

Not long after they achieve financial independence just investing in stocks as a renter, they're earning 3 times what they need to be financially independent with their 10 rentals.

But, this is about Monte Carlo modeling, so what if we did vary property appreciation rates, rent appreciation rates, inflation, mortgage interest rates and the stock market rate of return?

It is important to realize that because the property prices vary with each run sometimes the properties they're buying can be slightly more or less expensive. On average though, property prices are going up at about 3% per year.

Rent is similar. Rents can go up or down, but overall, rents are increasing by about 3% per year.

Mortgage interest rates started at about 8.5% for a non-owner-occupant loan without paying significant points. But, mortgage interest rates can get better—or worse—over time as they're acquiring properties. That means sometimes properties will cash flow better and sometimes they'll cash flow a little worse.

Let's look at their journey to financial independence buying ten 20% down payment rentals in Error! Reference source not found..

You can see there are times when the market goes in their favor (both the real estate and stock market) they achieve financial independence early. And, there are times when they still don't quite achieve it through 60 years.

How does it compare to the two previous strategies: renting and investing exclusively in stocks and buying an owner-occupant property and exclusively investing in stocks? See Error! Reference source not found..

It is getting harder to see what is happening in the chart as we add additional comparisons.

We can make it easier in two different ways. First, we can look at the same chart, but turn off the shaded areas for each strategy.

This would leave just the median—or the middle-most result—where half of them are better and half are worse. That's Error! Reference source not found..

This chart doesn't show up the range of results (how early or late they achieve FI) but it does show how much more they're likely to earn by buying the rentals by what percent of their financial independence goal they're earning.

By earning a higher percentage of the amount they need to be financially independent, they're able to support a higher standard of living.

In other words, if they needed to be earning $10,000 per month passively to be considered financially independent, but their earning 200% of that—or $20,000 per month—they could live at a much higher standard of living on $20,000 per month than the $10,000 per month that they needed—at a minimum—to be considered financially independent.

The second way to make it easier to see what is happening is looking at the percentage of the 1,000 runs that achieved financial independence like we did previously. That's Error! Reference source not found..

Buying ten 20% down payment rentals sees them achieving financial independence earlier (more left on the chart above) and then has a similar success rate to what they'd see if they bought an owner-occupant and invested in stocks.

Owner-Occupant, Rentals and Stocks

I think you know what's coming next: what if they bought an owner-occupant property with 5% down, then bought up to nine more rental properties, each with 20% down payments and invested the rest in stocks?

With static assumptions that's about 3.5 years faster than just renting and buying ten 20% down payment rentals. See Error! Reference source not found..

If we do Monte Carlo modeling, it looks like Error! Reference source not found..

Doing a very busy version of this chart by comparing it to the other strategies so far, it looks like Error! Reference source not found..

If we just look at the 50th percentile (median) value for the four options as seen in Error! Reference source not found..

It shows that buying the owner-occupant property and nine 20% down payment rentals appears to be faster and gives them a higher standard of living than even buying ten 20% down payment rentals.

If we look at the percentage of the 1,000 runs for reach strategy that achieved financial independence and when, we can see that buying an owner-occupant property and then nine 20% down rentals is the best performer yet as seen in Error! Reference source not found..

In the chart above you can see that not only does financial independence tend to happen faster (a little to the left on the chart), it also tends to be more consistent (a higher percentage of the runs achieve FI).

Nomad™ Real Estate Investing Strategy Example

There's so much more we could do with this, but for now I'll wrap it up with a slight curve ball.

Instead of buying an owner-occupant property and then buying nine 20% down payment rentals, let's imagine they Nomad™.

- They buy an owner-occupant property with 5% down payment.
- They live there for *at least* a year. That's a requirement of the lender to get an owner-occupant loan with an owner-occupant down payment and owner-occupant mortgage interest rate.

- Once their year is up AND they've saved up enough for another 5% down payment, they buy another owner-occupant property and move into it.
- They take the previous property they were living in and convert it to a rental property
- They repeat this until they have 9 rentals and the property they're living in

Instead of having to save up for 20% down payments, they acquire the same nine rental properties with only 5% down on each by moving into each one as an owner-occupant.

Is this better? Is this more probable for them to be financially independent? Is this faster to financial independence? Does this give a higher standard of living than the other strategies so far? And—we won't cover it here because it is a longer discussion—but is it more or less risky?

It turns out that with static assumptions (not Monte Carlo modeling yet), Nomad™ is 58 months (almost 5 years) faster to financial independence. See Error! Reference source not found..

If we add variability and do Monte Carlo modeling, we can look at how the Nomad™ strategy performs in Error! Reference source not found..

Brace yourself for the busy version comparing them all at the same time in Error! Reference source not found..

And, if we turn off the range of results and just look at the middle most (median) of the 1,000 runs for each strategy, we can see the following in Error! Reference source not found..

Still a bit busy to see what is going on, but I will point out, in the chart above, the Nomad™ strategy seems to give them the fastest achievement of financial independence and highest standard of living.

Isn't it interesting.

If we look at the percentage of the 1,000 runs that achieve financial independence and by when you can see even better in Error! Reference source not found..

The Nomad™ strategy achieves financial independence earliest (to the left on the chart above). It also has a higher probability of being financially independent earlier.

Additional Modeling

Now that we know the importance of considering the variability that might occur in the future, this is really just the beginning.

There is a ridiculous amount more to dig into here. We've just barely scratched the surface.

There's a lot more to model.

For example, we could model each strategy you're considering seeing how each strategy performs:

- Buying long-term buy and hold rental properties (short-term rentals, medium-term rentals, student rentals, storage units, assisted living, apartments, etc)

- Buying properties utilizing creative financing (owner financing, wrap financing, loan assumptions, rent-to-owns, agreements for deed, subject-to)
- Variations on the Nomad™ strategy (Nomad™ by Proxy, Nomad™ with House Hacking, Nomad™ to Short-Term Rental, Nomad™ with Lease-Option Exits, *The Ultimate Real Estate Agent Retirement Plan™*)
- House Hacking and related strategies
- Short-Term Rentals and related strategies
- Flipping properties and related strategies
- BRRRR and related strategies
- And much, much more

Or, combining one or more of these strategies at the same time (fix and flipping while acquiring long-term or short-term rentals as an example) or sequentially (fix and flipping for 10 years then switch to buy and hold).

Or, we could test a wide assortment of variations to your strategy:

- More or less reserves (and its impact on both speed and risk)
- More or less down payment size up to buying properties for all cash
- Buying down interest rates or not
- Getting roommates or not (house hacking)
- Selling via lease-options versus with a real estate agent or for sale by owner
- Paying off properties early with extra cash flow versus not

- Doing cash out refinances to buy additional properties faster
- Buying properties and selling them when you could take the proceeds (after all expenses including taxes) and then investing that money in stocks, bonds or something else to be financially independent
- Buying more properties than you need and selling them to pay off properties when it means you'd be financially independent
- And much, much more

Not Just Financial Independence

When we do these models, it is important to consider more than just how fast you're able to get to financial independence—even though that's what we focused on here.

Sometimes it is about your standard of living once you are financially independent. Some strategies might just barely get you to your minimum required income to be financially independent. While others will give you far more each month than you initially stated you needed allowing you to live at a much higher standard of living than you originally required.

Sometimes, it is about measuring, comparing and ultimately minimizing risks. Some strategies are riskier than others. They might get you to financial independence, on average, 1 year faster, but there's a 20 times greater chance you'll run out of money by pursuing that strategy than another one that gets you to financial independence, on average, a year slower.

That all might be worth considering... especially for your own unique situation.

It is important for you to evaluate your own strategy utilizing Monte Carlo modeling to better understand how to achieve financial independence faster, easier, with higher probability of success, with a higher standard of living and with less overall risk.

Or, if you are going to ignore one or more of those things, deliberately and strategically choosing to ignore them with full knowledge of the consequences.

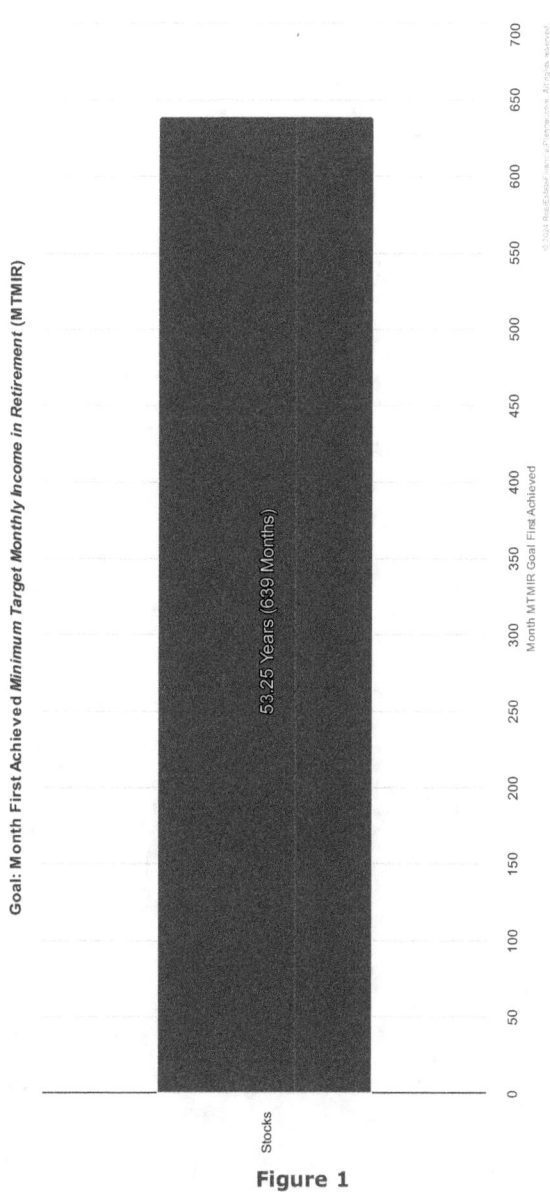

Figure 1

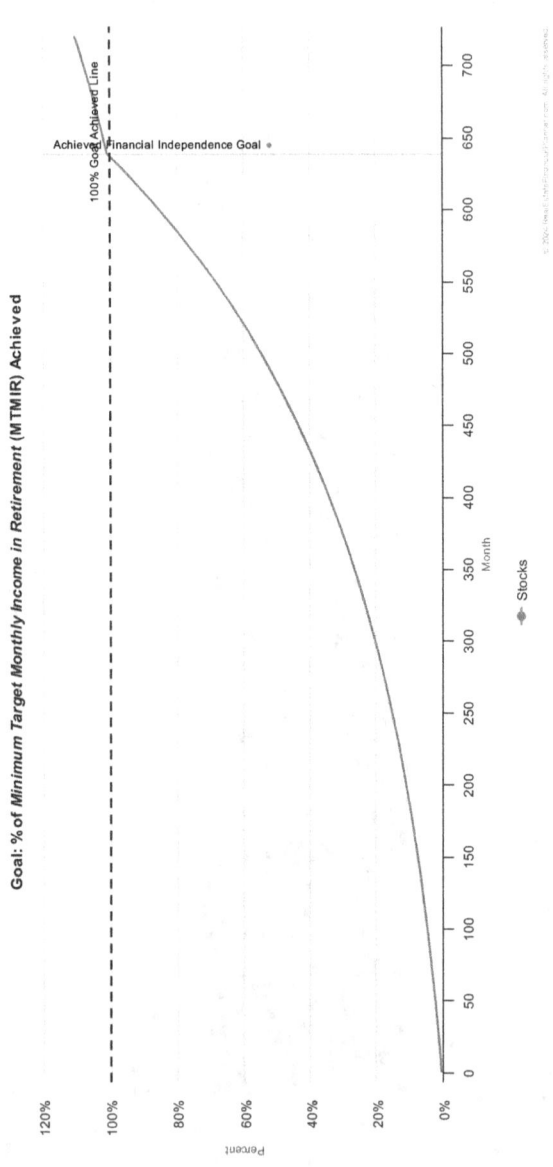

Figure 2

161

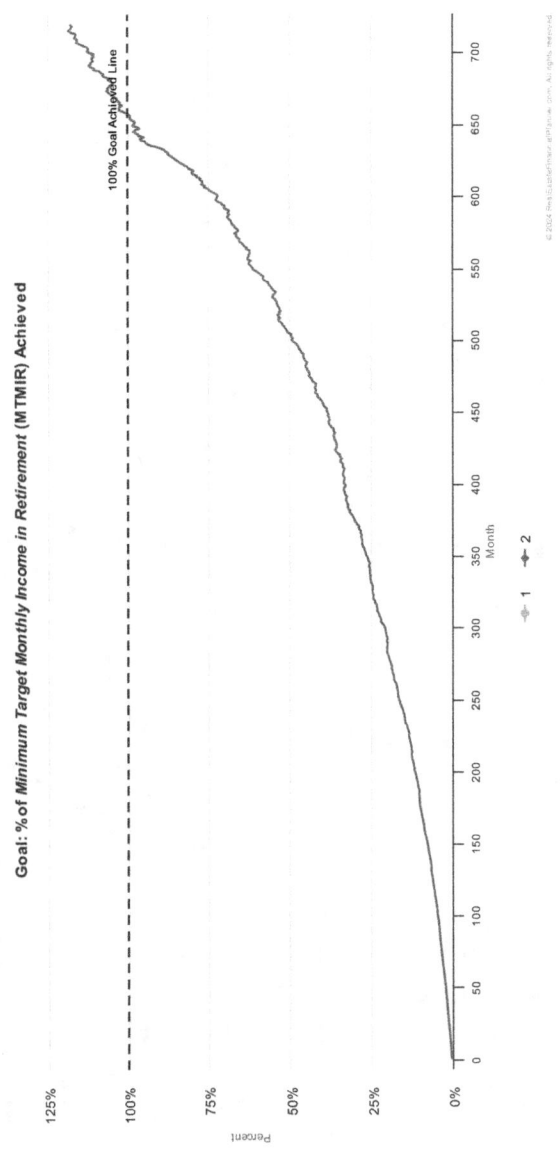

Figure 3

© 2024 James Orr. All rights reserved.

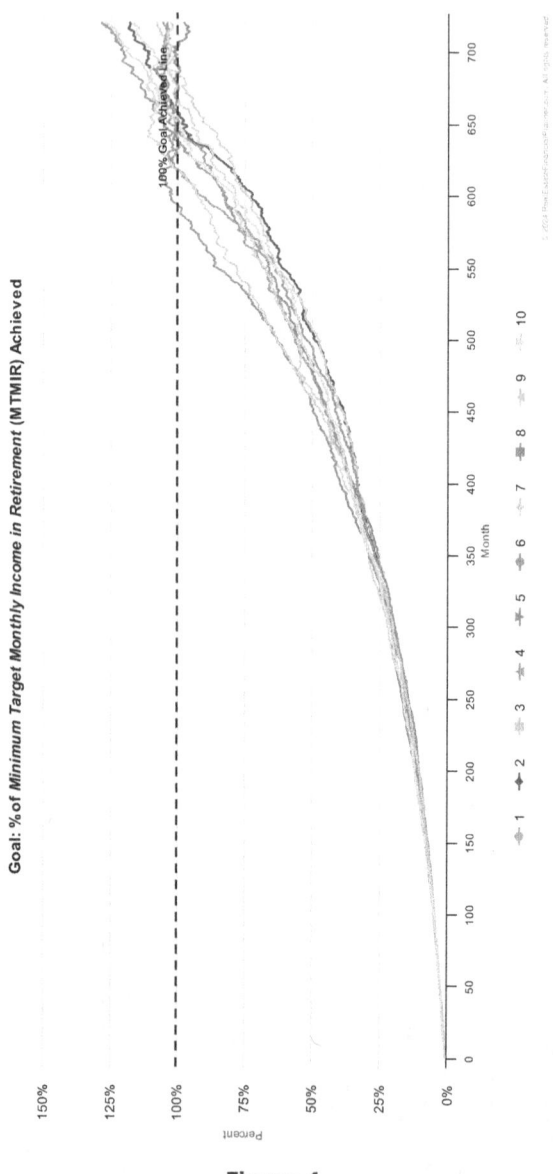

Goal: % of *Minimum Target Monthly Income in Retirement (MTMIR)* Achieved

Figure 4

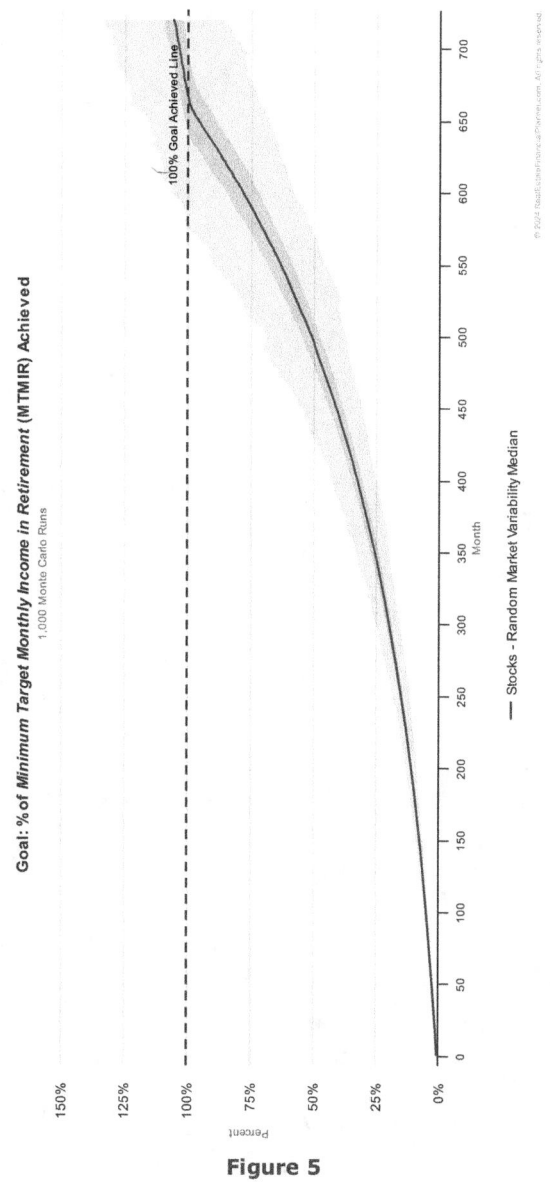

Figure 5

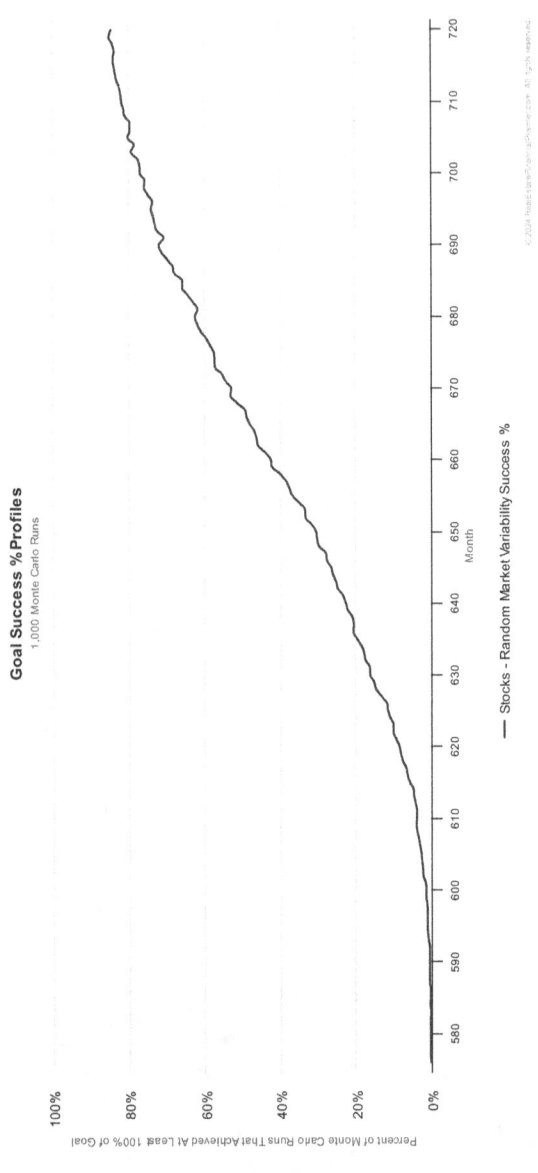

Figure 6

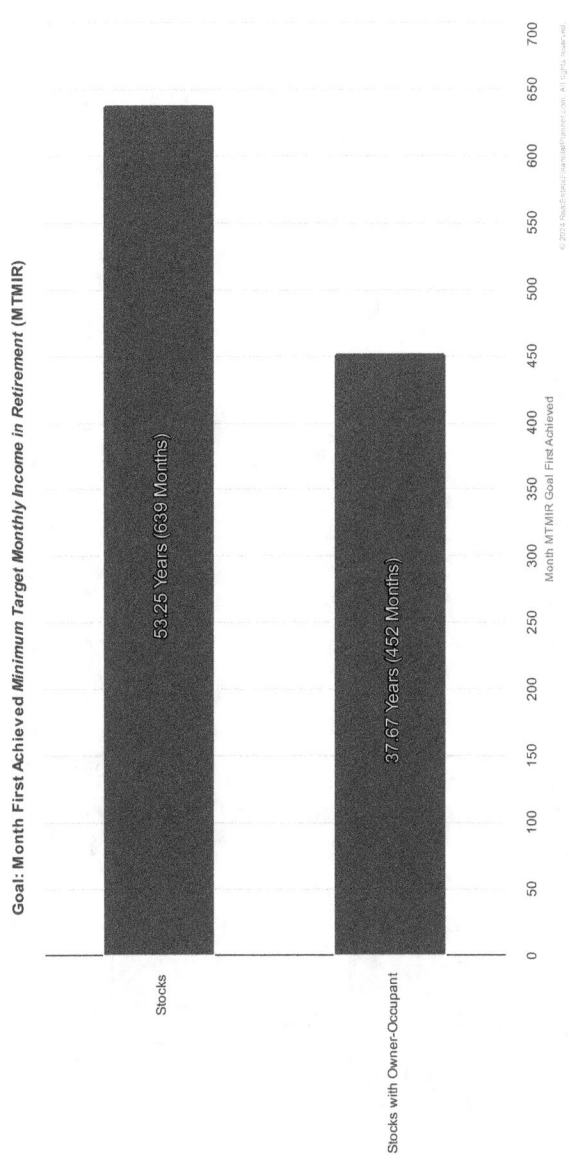

Figure 7

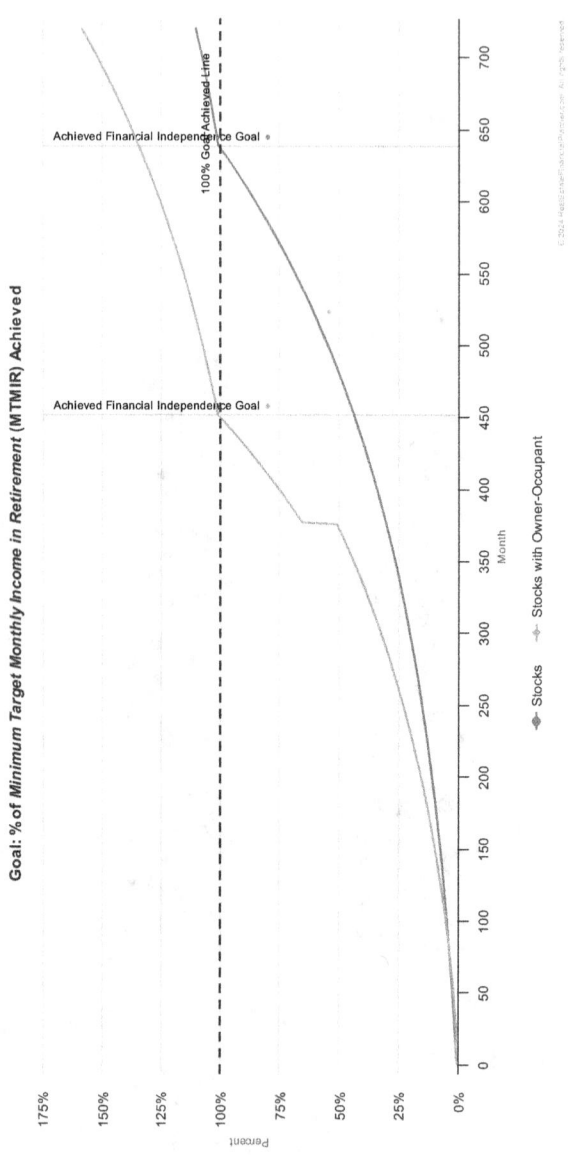

Figure 8

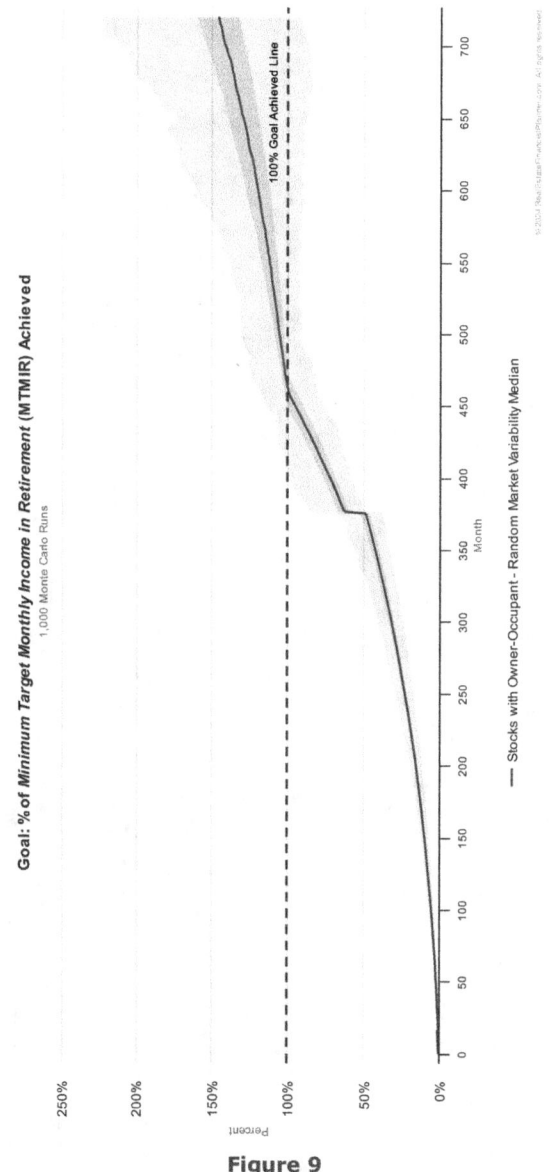

Goal: % of *Minimum Target Monthly Income in Retirement (MTMIR) Achieved*
1,000 Monte Carlo Runs

Figure 9

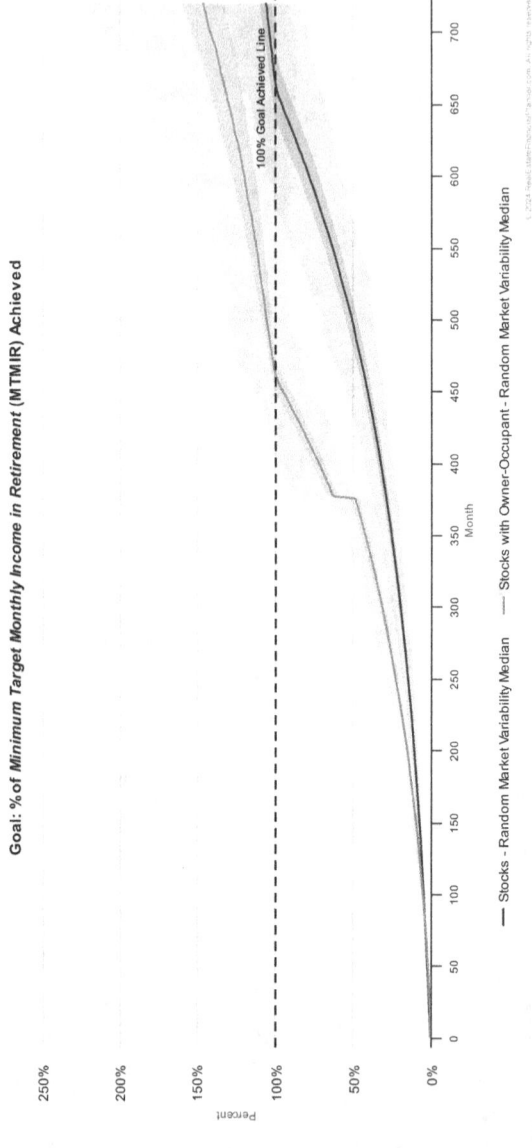

Goal: % of Minimum Target Monthly Income in Retirement (MTMIR) Achieved

Figure 10

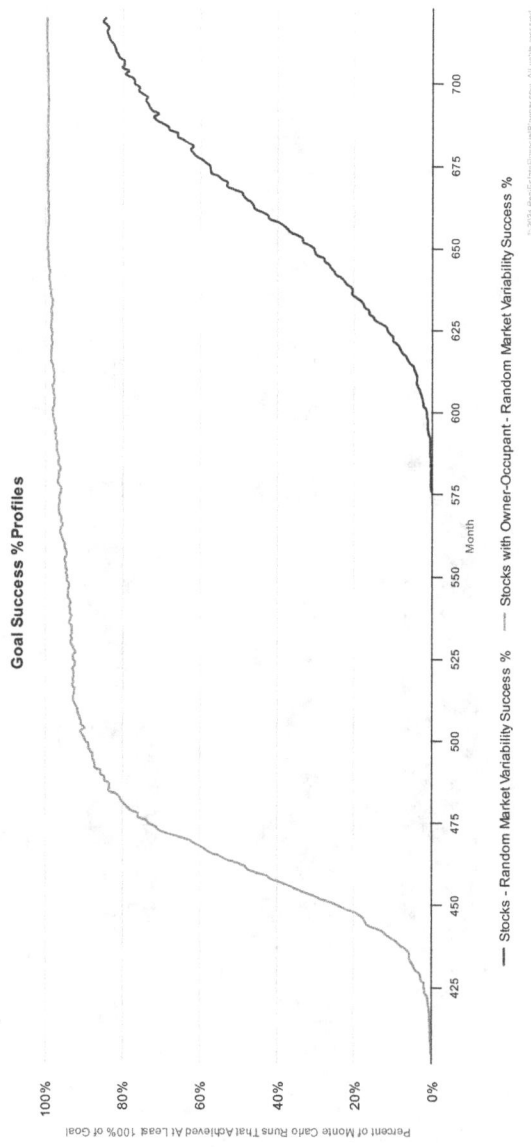

Figure 11

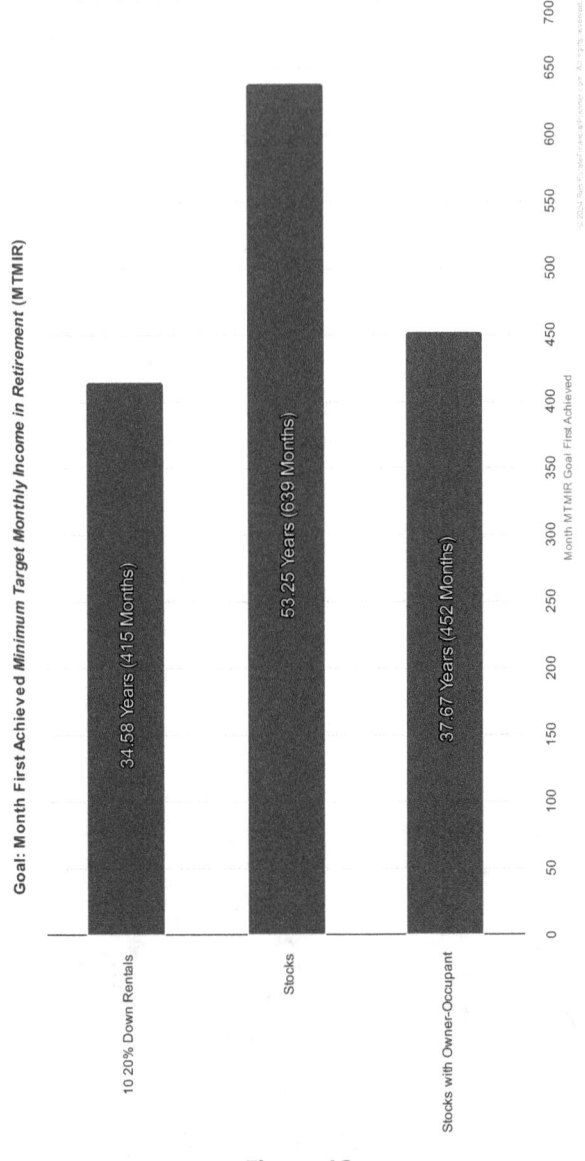

Figure 12

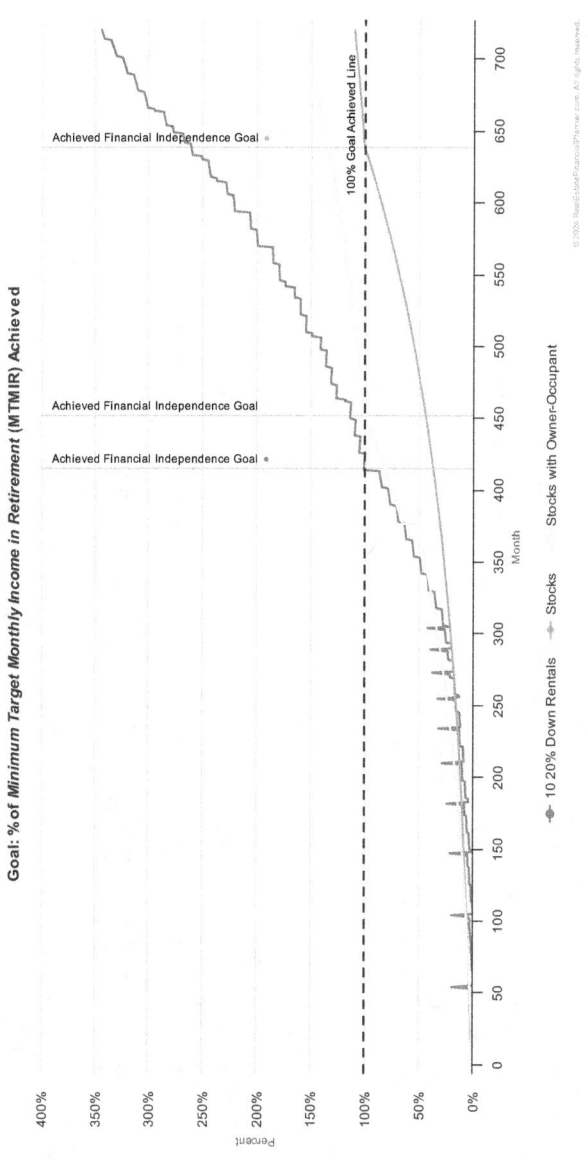

Figure 13

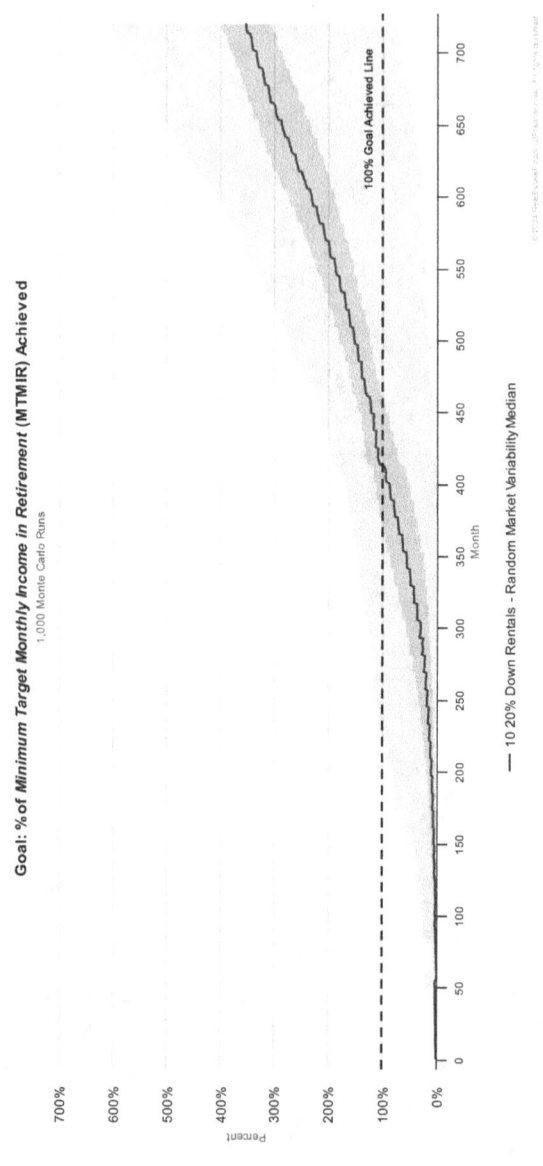

Goal: % of Minimum Target Monthly Income in Retirement (MTMIR) Achieved

1,000 Monte Carlo Runs

100% Goal Achieved Line

— 10 20% Down Rentals - Random Market Variability Median

Figure 14

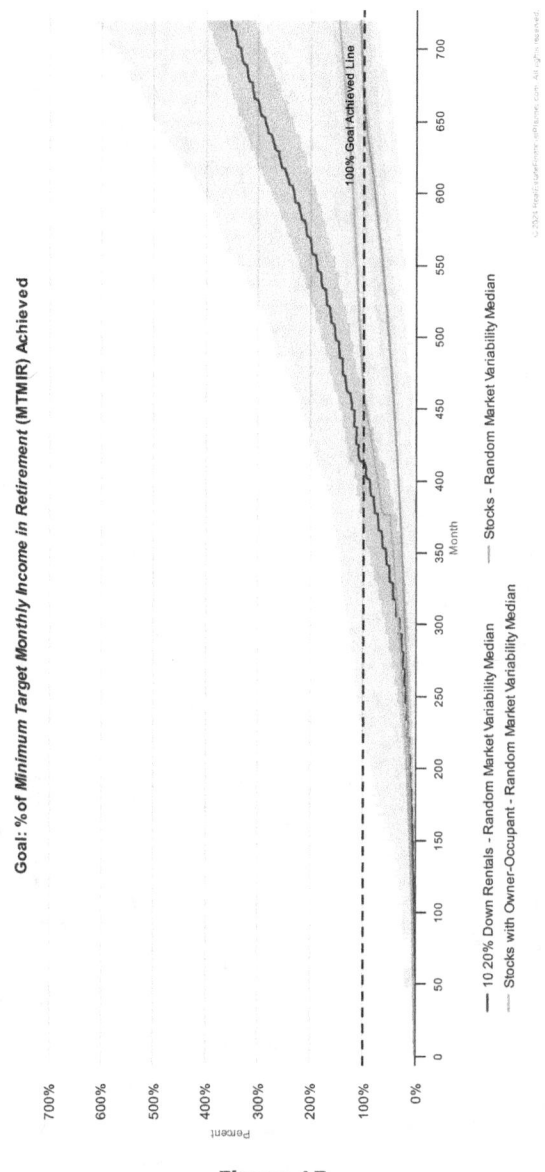

Figure 15

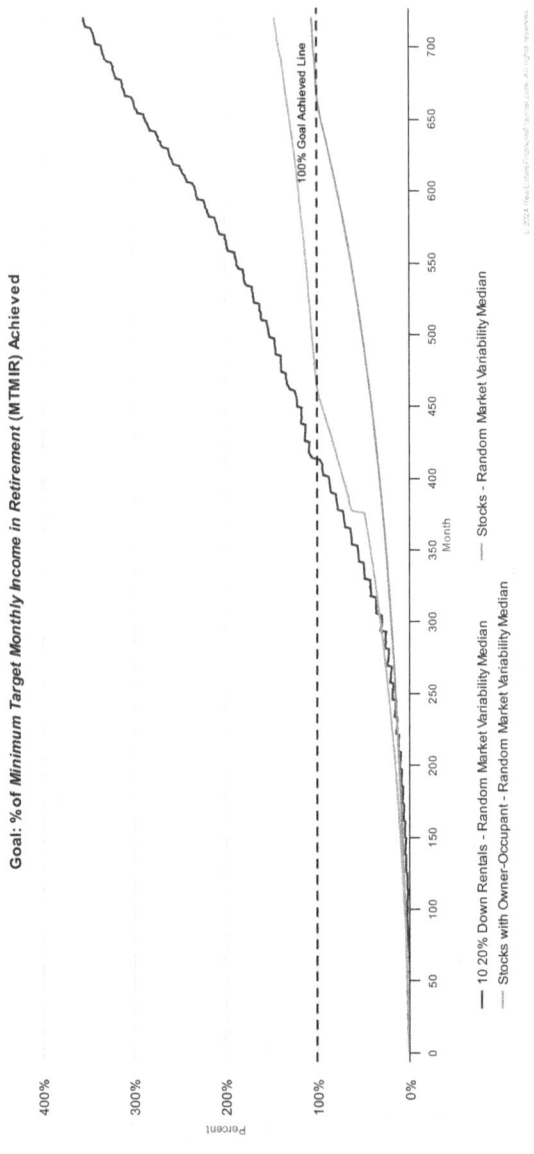

Figure 16

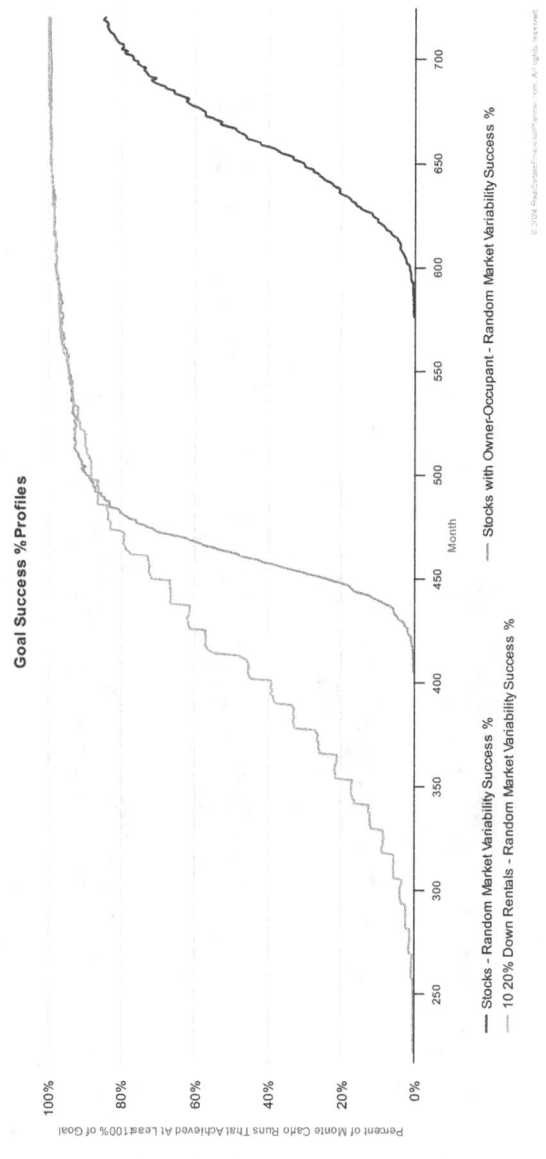

Figure 17

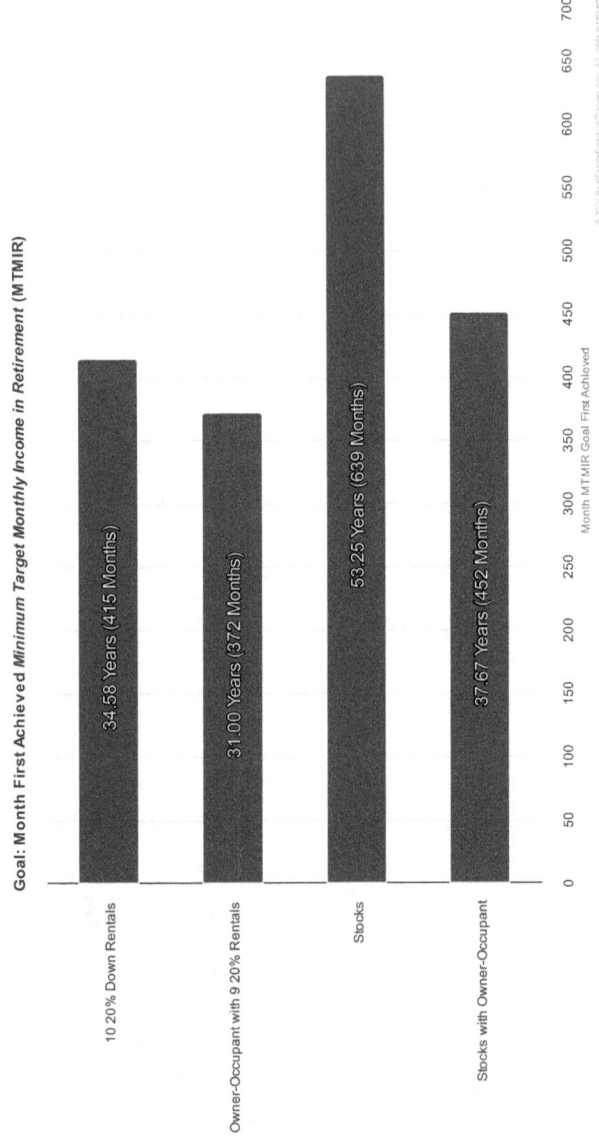

Figure 18

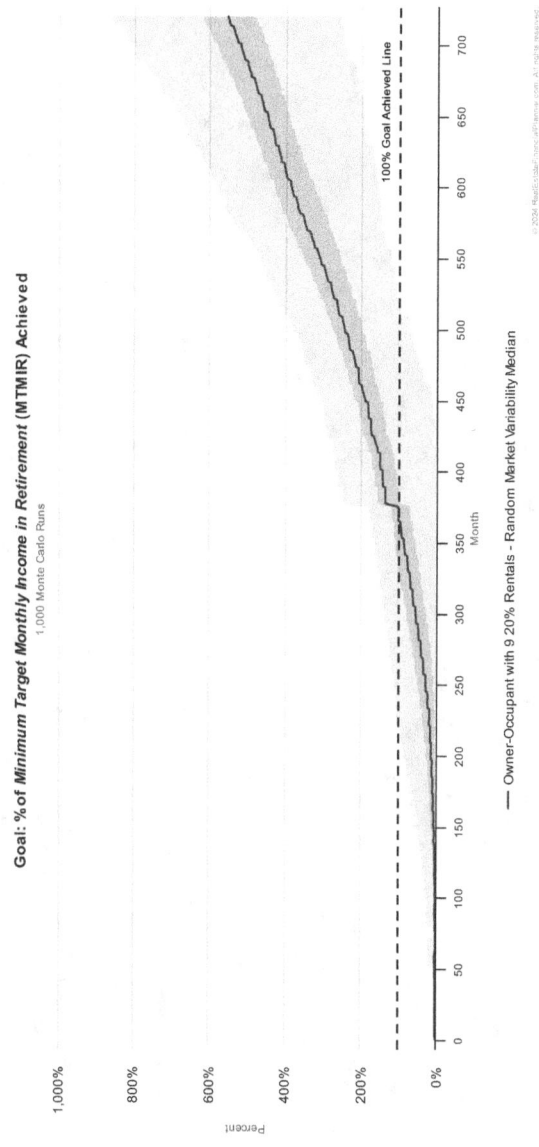

Figure 19

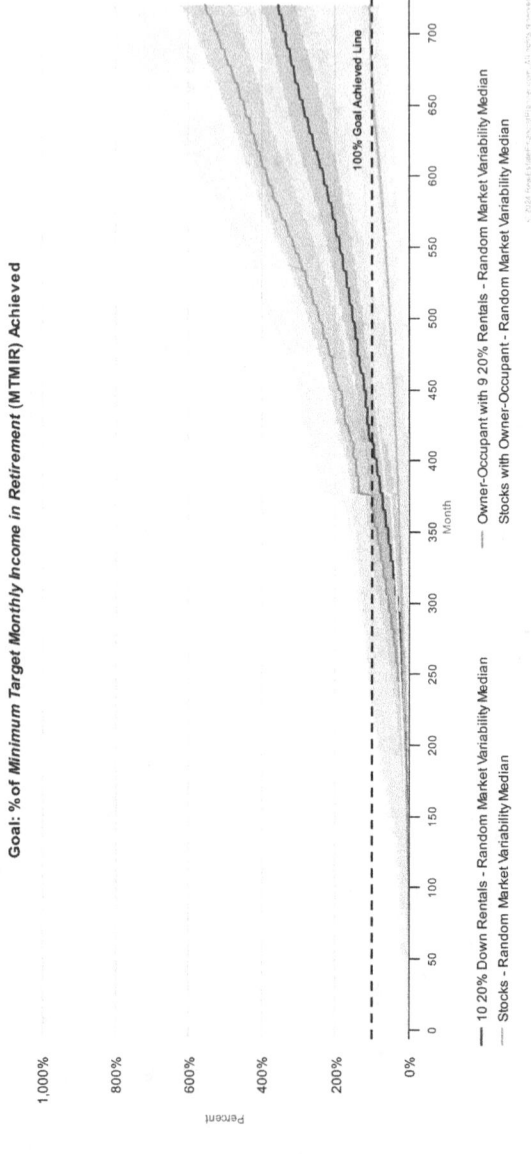

Figure 20

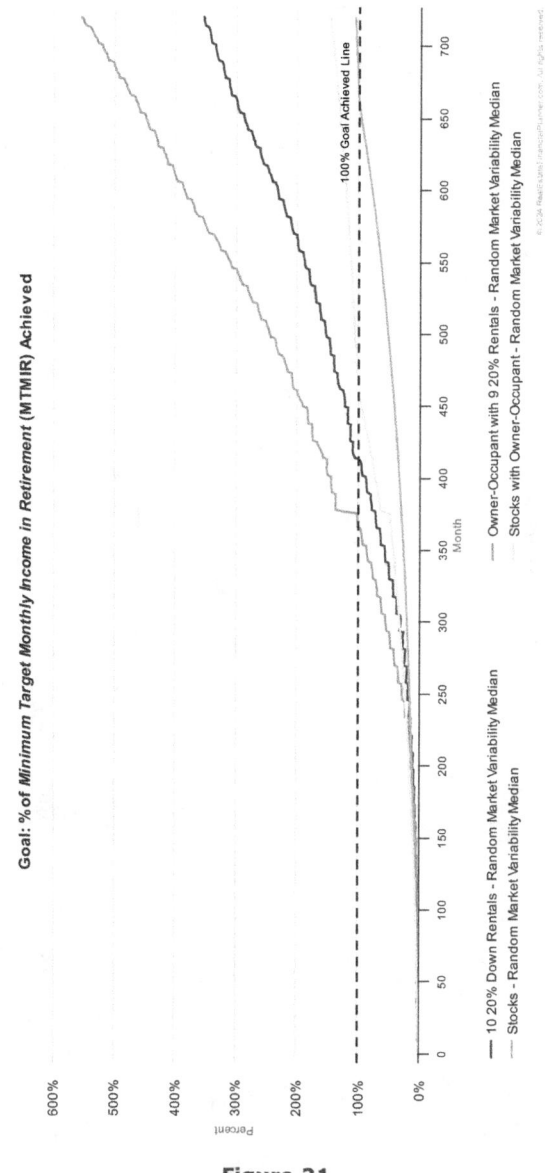

Figure 21

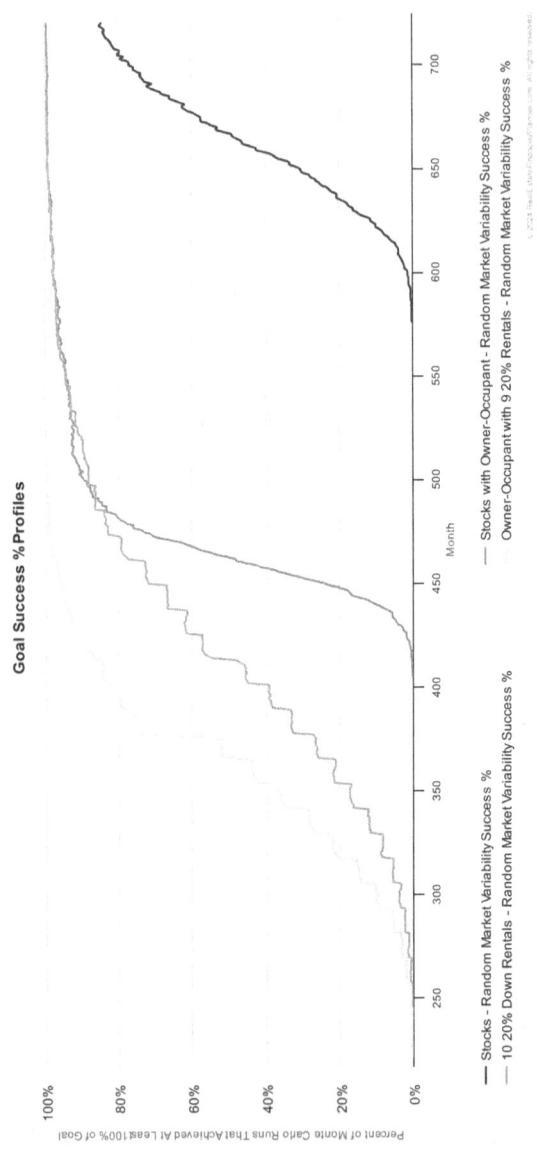

Figure 22

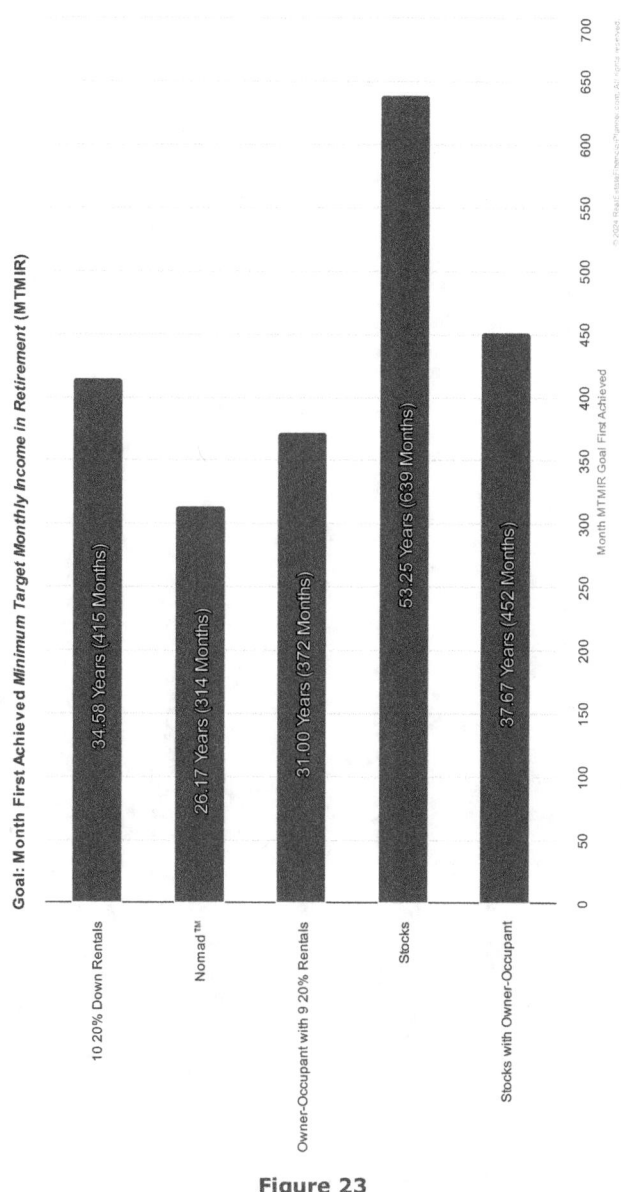

Figure 23

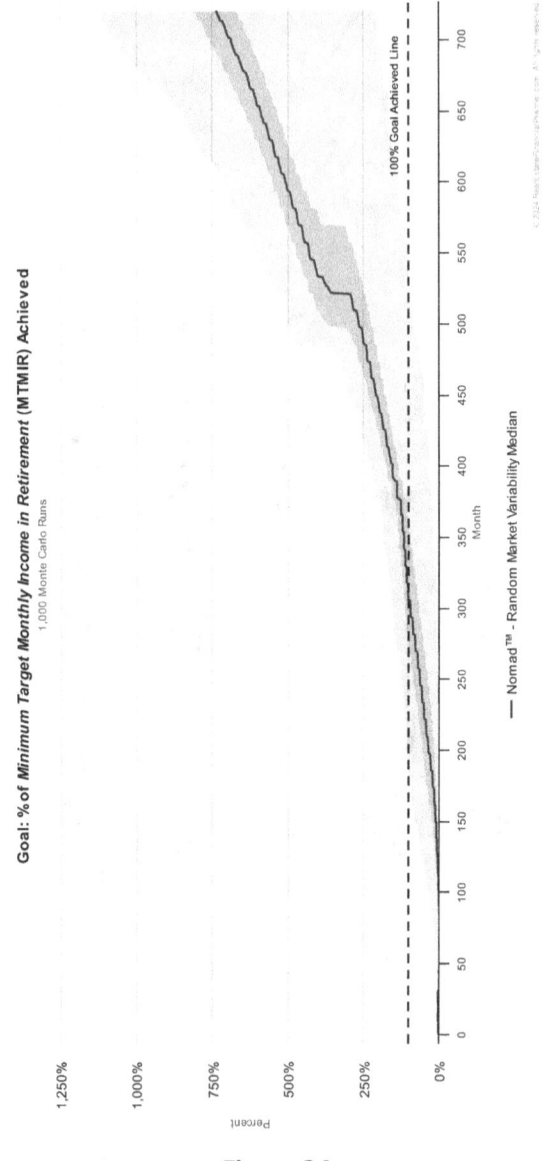

Goal: % of *Minimum Target Monthly Income in Retirement (MTMIR) Achieved*
1,000 Monte Carlo Runs

— Nomad™ - Random Market Variability Median

Figure 24

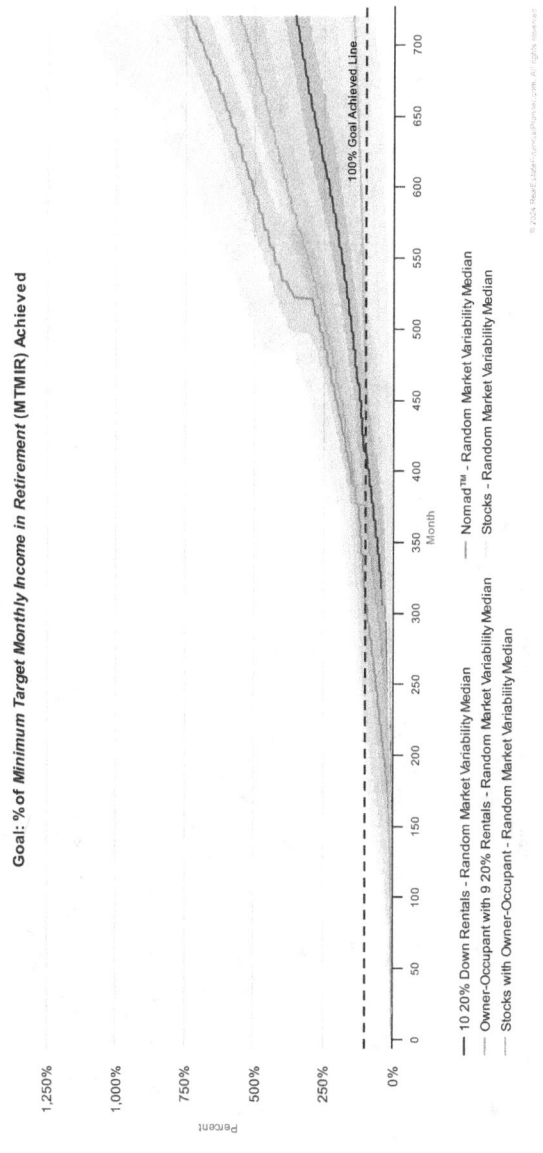

Goal: % of *Minimum Target Monthly Income in Retirement (MTMIR)* Achieved

Figure 25

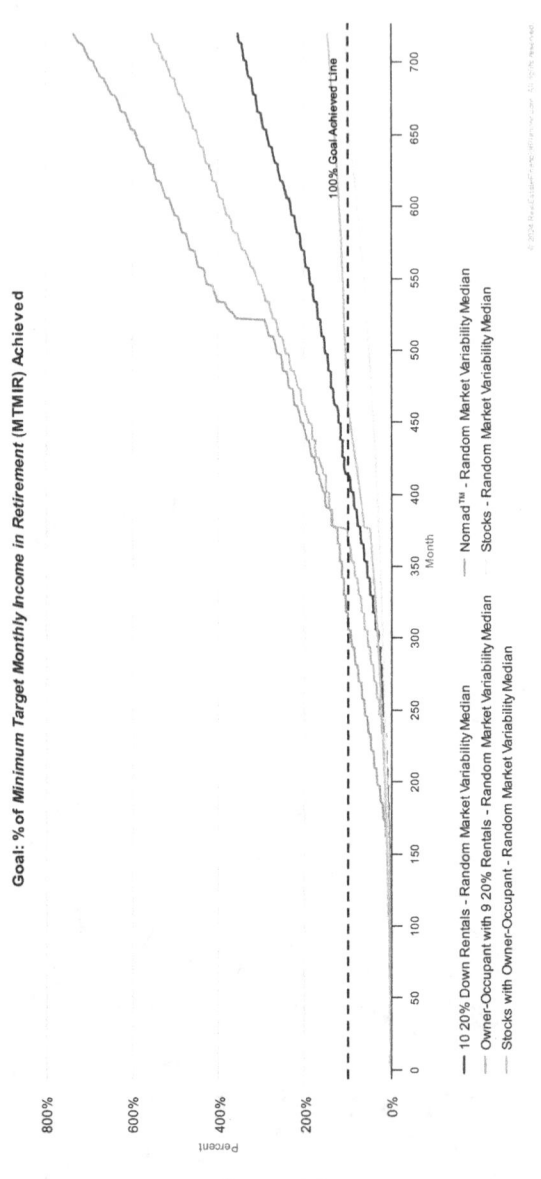

Figure 26

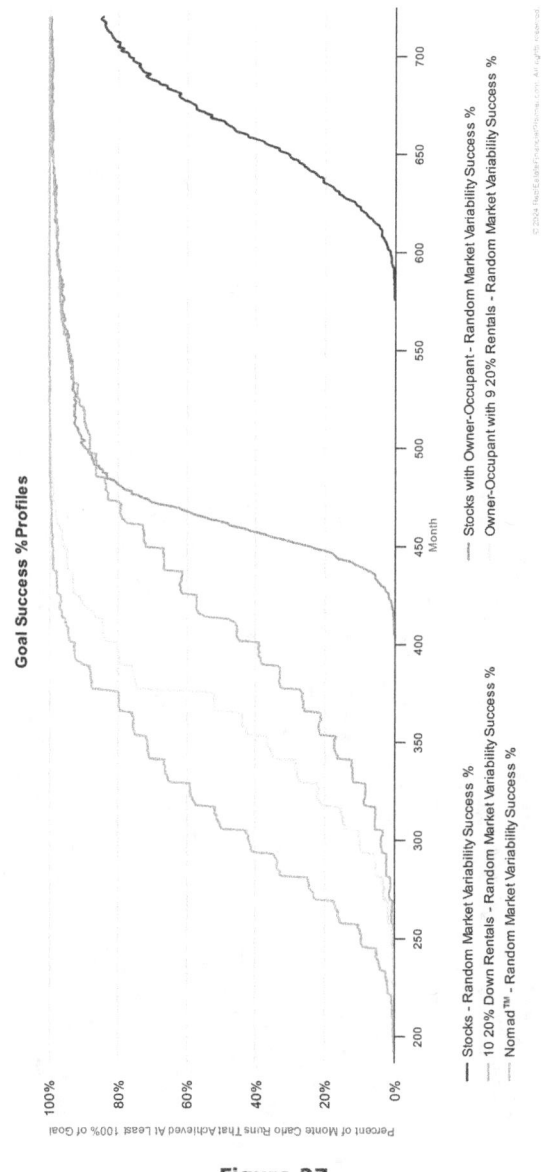

Figure 27

About the Author

James Orr is a seasoned real estate investor and the visionary creator of the Real Estate Financial Planner™ software. With a passion for sharing his wealth of knowledge, James has authored numerous books on real estate investing, covering a wide array of topics to help both novice and experienced investors succeed.

Living in Loveland, Colorado, James enjoys a fulfilling life with his wife, Tammy, whom he has been happily married to since 1995. Together, they have raised two grown sons. When he's not writing or managing his real estate investments, James is dedicated to teaching others the secrets of financial independence through smart property investments.

Also by James Orr

- The Real Estate Investing Mentor series of topic books
- How to Achieve Financial Independence and Live Your Passion Regardless of Age or Income: 10 Paths to Financial Independence Analyzed
- How to Acquire a Multi-Million Dollar Real Estate Portfolio With Just $3,000
- How to Acquire a Multi-Million Dollar Real Estate Portfolio Earning Just $5,000 Per Month
- Nomad™
- Ultimate Nomad™ Checklist
- Northern Colorado Real Estate Advisor
- Acquiring a Portfolio of Cash Flowing Properties In Northern Colorado: A Real Estate Financial Planner™ Blueprint
- Real Estate Investing Systems

Software and Spreadsheets

- Real Estate Financial Planner™ software
- The World's Greatest Real Estate Deal Analysis Spreadsheet™
- Should I Sell My Rental Property Spreadsheet™
- Should I Refinance My Rental Property Spreadsheet™
- CapEx Estimator for Rental Property – Basic and Advanced Spreadsheets
- Financial Independence Asset Allocation and Cash Flow Engines Spreadsheet™
- The Investor's Agent One-Page Business Plan™

A Small Request

Thank you for reading *The Real Estate Investing Mentor: The Affordable $50K Coaching Alternative* topic book on **Introduction to Creative Financing**.

I am positive if you follow what I've written, you will be on your way to successfully investing in real estate. When you do please reach out and share your story.

I have a small, quick favor to ask. Would you mind taking a minute or two and leaving an honest review for this book on Amazon?

Reviews are the BEST way to help others purchase this book and keep the price of my books low for everyone, and I check all my reviews looking for helpful feedback.

Please visit:

https://REFP.info/intro-creative-financing-book

Questions?

Thank you for taking the time to read this book. If a concept sparked a question or if you feel there's an area that could be explained more clearly, I'd truly appreciate hearing from you. You can reach me at **jamesorr@gmail.com** with any feedback specific to this title. My goal is to make each book as helpful and practical as possible, and your input plays a big part in that.

Just a note—while I'm here to help deepen your understanding of this book's topics, this isn't intended as a personal coaching service. For advice tailored to your own situation, I encourage you to work closely with a real estate agent who can provide the insight and support unique to your goals.

Thank you again for reading, and for helping me make this series an even better resource for investors like you.